Alex Nicol is a writer and broadcaster. He began his career with the ABC in 1967 as a trainee rural reporter. Two years later he became the producer and presenter of the national radio program *All Ways on Sunday* and later became the manager of ABC Orange.

He has worked as a jackeroo, as a sheep and wool officer for the New South Wales Department of Agriculture, as an agriculture college lecturer, and as the media liaison officer with the Australian Wheat Board.

Alex is also a playwright, and his plays have been produced in London, New York, Melbourne and Sydney, with credits including an award at the Royal Exchange Theatre, Manchester's International Writing Competition, the Wal Cherry Award, and The London International Playwriting Award. His play *Three Toe Scratch* was shortlisted for the Sydney Theatre Company's Patrick White Award.

Old Days, Old Ways

STORIES FROM MY
RADIO DAYS IN THE BUSH

ALEX NICOL

ALLEN&UNWIN
SYDNEY•MELBOURNE•AUCKLAND•LONDON

First published in 2019

Allen & Unwin
83 Alexander Street
Crows Nest NSW 2065
Australia
Phone: (61 2) 8425 0100
Email: info@allenandunwin.com
Web: www.allenandunwin.com

A catalogue record for this
book is available from the
National Library of Australia

ISBN 978 1 76052 849 2

Internal design by Bookhouse, Sydney
Set in 13.2/16 pt Spectrum MT by Bookhouse, Sydney
Printed and bound in Australia by Griffin Press

10 9 8 7 6 5 4 3 2 1

The paper in this book is FSC® certified.
FSC® promotes environmentally responsible,
socially beneficial and economically viable
management of the world's forests.

This book is dedicated to my wife, Diana. Like so many women of her generation she sacrificed her career to follow her husband. So many times while I was being feted as a 'star' she was at home busy raising our family.

CONTENTS

WELCOME TO THE FAMILY

2CR WAS ONE OF FIVE HUGE TRANSMITTERS THAT THE GOVERNMENT of the day set up in the 1930s to 'cover Australia'. And they very nearly did.

Corowa in southern New South Wales, Rockhampton on the coast in Queensland, and Crystal Brook in outback South Australia came on stream in 1932. 2CR, with her transmitter at Cumnock, in the centre of New South Wales, followed five years later. Her powerful signal meant that broadcasts from the studio in Orange could be heard as far north as the Queensland border and as far south as Victoria. The old girl had a big family.

I arrived at the station in 1967, a very raw trainee rural reporter. She saw me grow to present a three-and-a-half-hour national program from her transmitter, and eventually to become manager at a time when technology was changing and we were no longer in awe of that big stick out at Cumnock.

There were flowers in the house when we arrived. Irene Hatswell saw to that. Welcome to the family.

Neil Inall would teach me. He sat me in a 'dead studio'. I've never been comfortable with switches and dials, and what was in front of me terrified me. 'Talk to the microphone as a friend,' was his advice. 'You're not talking to people at a meeting; you're having a chat with a mate. And practise, practise, practise.

'Did you wash under your arms in the shower this morning? Of course you did, but you don't remember, do you? No. It's second nature. That's the way handling those switches and dials will become. They mustn't get in the way.'

I disappointed him so many times.

I am on my own controlling the breakfast session for the first time.

Think it through, I tell myself. Listen for the time call from Sydney, fade down the signal from Sydney, fade up our transmitter, open the microphone, make my announcements, close the microphone, fade up the control on the tape recorder that has this morning's interview.

That's not hard. But why isn't the interview going to air? Don't panic. Open the microphone and call the time. Press the start button on the recorder again. Why won't the interview go to air?

Very quietly the studio door opens. Pat Britten crosses noiselessly to the desk. He reaches over, closes the microphone, turns the tape recorder on, gives me an encouraging smile and says, 'Try again.'

It's got to be like washing your armpits.

Neil and I divided the territory. He'd take the stories west of Dubbo, I'd take the eastern half of the region, and we would travel. Oh, how we would travel. There was no such thing as a recorded telephone interview. If you wanted to talk with someone, then you drove and you met them face to face. We were often away from family overnight, over nights.

I was somewhere in the south of our country. They knew that, but where exactly? My mother-in-law had been killed in a car accident, and my wife, Diana, and our three young children were at home alone. Neil was doing the breakfast show and asked our listeners to find me. One of them managed the motel where I was sleeping. 'Please ring the station straight away.'

I'd been with the ABC for perhaps six months, at 2CR for perhaps three months, but when I got back to the studio the manager sat me down. 'You're going to need some time off. Don't

2CR's transmitter at Cumnock. The old lady was meant to cover one-fifth of Australia.

worry about that. Take as much as you need.' He opened the safe. 'And you'll need some money.' He handed some over. 'We'll work it out later.'

Welcome to the family.

DEAR OLD M

EACH MORNING WHEN I CAME INTO THE STUDIO, ON MY DESK WOULD BE a neat pile of copy paper. At the top of the first page I would see the typed words: *'This is the news, written by Laurie Mulhall, read by . . .'* Dear Old M claimed authorship, and you had better do his words justice. The copy was there in plenty of time for me to read it, reread it aloud and get it right.

Laurie Mulhall—Dear Old M—was a masterful journalist with a poetic turn of phrase. On slow news days I would announce to our listeners, 'Following last week's rain, green shoots of new life spike the rich earth of the wheat country of the Central West.' You wouldn't get that in the *Tele*.

Dear Old M, our journalist in charge, was something of a father figure. He was 'Dear Old' because no matter who he was referring to, they became 'Dear Old'. Hence Neil Inall was 'Dear Old I' and Colin Munroe, who'd done time at the station as a rural reporter, was 'Dear Old Bangers and Mash'.

He'd sit in the newsroom, headphones clamped to his head and, in the early days, a pipe smouldering beside him. He had a marvellous habit of tap, tapping on the space bar of his typewriter as he encouraged the story out of whichever of our far-flung correspondents was on the phone. He didn't take notes; he crafted the story as it was being told to him so that clean copy was the inevitable result.

Dear Old M, Laurie Mulhall second from the left, part poet. . . 'Following last week's rain green shoots of new life spike the rich earth of the wheat country of the Central West' . . . master journalist.

Mrs Mac was our Trangie correspondent and a story in her own right. The wife of the local doctor—who'd come to town as a locum and, in *Saturday Evening Post* style, just stayed—she was known by, and knew, everyone for a hundred miles around.

I listened in horrified fascination once as she reported on a gruesome local accident.

'Two boys, Mrs Mac?' asked Dear Old M. *Tap, tap, tap.* 'And they drove under the fence?' he repeated. *Tap, tap.* 'And the windscreen was down? . . . Oh, it was a jeep. There wasn't any windscreen?' *Tap.* 'Oh, that's good, Mrs Mac . . . And it what? Cut one boy's head off? Right off?' *Tap, tap, tap.* 'Actually decapitated him? Oh, that's good, Mrs Mac, that's good. It was barbed wire? Oh, good, good.'

Getting accurate, sympathetic copy from a conversation like that is a rare skill.

Only a graded journalist was permitted to write the news copy, but 2CR had a big area to cover, and on more than one occasion a major national story meant that it was all hands to the pump.

There'd been a mine disaster at Cobar, and head office rang to suggest that someone should pop out to cover the story. It was a lazy 530 miles there and back; those were the days before they would 'chopper' someone to cover a dog fight. Besides, there were other stories to be covered, so we wouldn't be doing that.

I asked if I could help. M was trying to raise the mine management and told me to get onto our Cobar correspondent, stay on the phone and get anything I could. Our correspondent was, often as not, a local housewife with an interest in seeing that her town got its share of news, and that was the case at Cobar. They certainly weren't going to make a fortune selling news tips to the ABC.

I rang. At the other end the receiver was jerked off its cradle and a voice snarled, 'Who's that?'

I introduced myself and was met with: 'You ought to have more sense. *Blue Hills* is on.' Crash.

I should say that someone was supposed to keep an ear to the daily broadcast of the hugely popular rural drama *Blue Hills*. Inevitably, someone who'd missed the show would ring after lunch to be brought up to date with the goings on at Tanimbla. Get your perspective right, boy!

When M or his assistant took leave, they'd be replaced by a Sydney-based reporter who, wasn't thrilled at the opportunity to work in the bush. Obviously, they had no personal knowledge of the district, and that could lead to some accidental misreporting. Diplomatic handling was required.

'Sixteen feet of water covered the Bedgerabong Road.' I read. If there was sixteen feet of water over any road on the flat plains of the Central West, it was already too late for Noah to get involved. 'Er, perhaps sixteen inches?' I suggested.

'Feet. Definitely feet.' Was the response.

So I fudged a bit.

Came a day when M was ill and there was no replacement. What was the alternative? No news?

I hesitantly asked if he would trust me to put out a bulletin and got his blessing. I knew he'd be listening from his sickbed and I was proud of my effort.

When he returned, he chided me. 'What happened to the urn story, Nic?'

The CWA branch in one of our tiniest towns had raised the money to buy a new urn, and the fact had been dutifully reported by our correspondent.

'There wasn't room for it, M.'

'What, not four lines?' he insisted.

'Really, M. It's not much of a story,' was my best excuse.

'To you, Nic. Not to them.'

THE FIRST TIME

You never forget the first time, especially if it was a disaster. Nineteen sixty-nine was a very good year for red wine, and Australia was in the early stages of its love affair with the grape. It had been a long and difficult courtship.

There had been some early romances. Those German vine dressers came by special invitation of the South Australian government. The boardrooms of England decreed the building of mini chateaus (very mini) in northern Victoria, and Colin Campbell—of Rutherglen fame—told me that time was when the local winemakers would load a keg on the back of a cart and sell their produce by the billy-full to the local goldminers cooking Sunday lunch over their campfires.

Even our boys had done their bit. Don't tell me that 'plonk' isn't the result of some blushing, tongue-tied young Anzac trying to order *vin blanc* from a comely maid, but the wine had gone sour.

Wine bars were dark, gloomy places frequented by the flotsam of society in search of fourpenny dark, and those English gentlemen grew tired of the robust colonial reds . . . calling it 'Emu wine' probably wasn't the smartest marketing strategy. Australian table wine was on the nose; only the strong survived.

Jack Roth was a survivor. The name says it all. Jack's antecedents were those pioneering German winemakers looking for the right side of the hill to plant their vines in Australia, and they chose Mudgee. I jackerooed at Mudgee. I married a Mudgee girl from an old Mudgee family. I knew Jack and Jack knew me. He would be my first interviewee in my new profession of rural journalism.

It seems sacrilegious to say it now, but Jack was surviving by selling his grapes as table grapes. But he had an ace in the hole: he made rummy port. He matured his port in rum barrels. The result was unique. It was famous and it was good. I'd have Jack tell me the secret of rummy port.

This was my first interview and I was very careful. Recorder level was checked and rechecked before I began the interview with 'Mr Roth'. Naturally, we were in the cellars; equally naturally, Mr Roth was at pains to demonstrate his techniques as the interview progressed.

'These were the barrels. They came from America,' said Mr Roth. 'Here, try this.' And he handed me a generous glass of first-year-in-the-barrel wine. 'It was a mistake. I wanted the traditional brandy casks.'

This was great stuff. I checked that the tape was still recording . . . Yes, everything looked fine.

Mr Roth and I sat beside one of those barrels and sipped the contents as we chatted.

'It's the time the wine stands in the casks that makes the difference,' I was assured. 'Now, this has been down for a couple of years. Try this.'

We moved to a new cask and took up station there. The sipping and the discussion of techniques grew animated. 'Mr Roth' vanished, his place taken by 'Jack', and the secrets of the winemaker's craft began to flow as freely as the rummy port.

I distinctly remember—at least, I think I do—deciding that I'd better put another tape on the recorder. This stuff was too good to miss.

Jack and I eventually parted the best of friends, with me promising solemnly that I'd call him with the date and time of this magnificent broadcast. He handed me a bottle of the best rummy port—'a gift for Diana'.

The drive from Mudgee to Orange has never been easy, but the return trip on this occasion was particularly difficult.

Recording an interview is one thing; editing it to make a program is a different tipple altogether. I sat down faced with the prospect of turning an hour of interview into a five-minute broadcast.

Only then did I discover that something was amiss.

The longer the interview went, the stranger the voices seemed. By what can only have been some curious fault in the recorder, consonants and vowels collided with each other, making the speech hopelessly blurred.

This was a tragedy! My first interview with the ABC, a groundbreaking exposé of the secrets of rummy port, was ruined because of a technical failure. What was I going to tell 'Mr Roth'?

TOUCH AND GO

THE AUTUMN WAS WET, VERY WET. THE COUNTRY HAD BEEN WORKED UP, but unless the rain stopped, we weren't going to get the wheat crop sown. You just couldn't get a tractor and machinery onto the ground. That great rain would be wasted.

Never let it be said that farmers are not inventive. The rice crop is flown into waterlogged paddies, so let's fly the wheat crop in.

Hazeltons, flying out of the Cudal airport, had a well-established top-dressing and aerial-spraying business; they were also pioneers when it came to aerial firefighting. They were up for the job. Several local farmers had already used them to get the crop in. Hazeltons were now refining the technique, and I wanted to know how it was being done. I was keen to go up with a pilot and experience it firsthand. As always, Hazeltons were cooperative; all I had to do was present myself at Cudal.

Now, I'd experienced flying in light aircraft before, and reckoned I had the technique of recording in that noisy atmosphere down pat. Just turn the microphone input down very low and hold the mic right against your lips. It gives you clear voice against the background of the aircraft noise—perfect. And if I wanted comment from the pilot? Just ask the question, leave a break and put the mic close to his lips. Easy.

When I got to Cudal I was a bit disappointed. I wouldn't be going up with a pilot actually sowing a crop; someone else would take me up to 'observe'. As we taxied for take-off, I noticed a badly dented crop duster minus a wing at the side of the strip.

'Ouch! Who did that?'

'Me.'

'Ah—what happened?'

'Just touched a corner post.'

'Landing?'

'No, turning at the end of a run.'

'Oh. You okay?'

'Yeah. You're never in trouble so long as you keep flying.'

Flying the crop in, I was to learn, was done at about the same height as crop spraying. To put it into perspective, the aircraft needed to lift a fraction to go over the fence at the end of a run. I expected that, as 'observers', we'd fly high over the paddock while the bloke below us did the job.

Not a bit of it. My pilot settled in at perhaps 10 feet above the plane sowing the crop and followed him up and down the paddock. All I can really remember is the sickening feeling in the pit of my stomach as we lifted, turned and dipped at the end of each run. I did remember to turn the tape recorder on but, strangely, when I got back to the studio there was nothing on it but the sound of the aircraft. I hadn't said a word.

Back home, I laid over the sound of the aircraft a riveting description of how the job was done. Hear that? I was there on the job.

TECHNICIAN MAGIC

'Have a try at this.'

'This' was a piece of cable with a post office jack at one end and two little bulldog clips at the other, and it was being offered by one of the Postmaster-General's Department technicians who kept an eye on things technical at 2CR. I didn't have the faintest idea what it might do. We were technical virgins inheriting Postmaster-General technology.

Tucked away in the record library at 2CR was a big 78 rpm shellac disc without a label. Curiosity must be satisfied, so I sat it on a turntable and dropped the pick-up arm into place—only to see it immediately rejected. It took a couple more tries before the penny dropped that with this record the pick-up arm started in the centre of the disc and worked towards the outside.

What I had was a recording of an interview between an unnamed reporter and someone from the Department of Agriculture extolling the virtues of superphosphate. It was an early field recording from the times when Aunty ABC would send a recording van out into the bush for just such an interview. It would have been a full day's adventure with what was then cutting-edge technology.

Sitting beside me on the console desk in the studio was a set of chimes. If you're old enough, you just might remember the melodious *bong, bong, bong* that issued periodically for no apparent reason during ABC broadcasts. The chimes were a signal that a switch between ABC networks was about to take place.

Now, when any ten-year-old can whip out a handheld device to record whatever action takes his fancy and then instantly transmit it to his friends, it all sounds terribly quaint.

Broadcasts from 2CR's Orange studio could be picked up as far away as St George, in Queensland, and down on the Victorian border, but, for all practical purposes, it covered an area perhaps 500 miles east to west, and 300 miles north to south.

If you wanted to cover a story anywhere in that wide sweep of New South Wales, there was only one way: drive to meet the subject, then interview them and drive back. You spent a lot of time on the road. There was no legal technology available for recording a telephone conversation. It was possible to use a nasty suction cap on the back of a receiver device, but the quality was terrible, and anyway it was illegal to record a telephone conversation.

The ABC had two standard portable tape recorders. The Nagra was a heavy but beautiful machine that was (and is) absolutely bulletproof, and that provided magnificent recording quality. And then there was the Stelavox, a particularly nasty piece of work nicknamed the 'Stelavixen'. It was light but equipped with only a three-inch tape; consequently, you had about three to four minutes of recording time. It certainly focused your attention on getting to the crux of the story. It also had the frustrating habit of running out of battery power at a critical moment, so you often finished up with a variable speed recording and some strange voice reproduction.

'I reckon this'll let you turn any telephone into a landline.' It was our friendly tech, wiggling his bit of cable and bulldog clips at me.

A 'landline' was the standard way of sending a recording from one ABC studio to another while retaining the sound quality. In effect, it meant dedicating a particular telephone line to the task, and keeping all other 'calls' off it.

'You could ring from Bourke, attach this to your recorder and you'd get broadcast-quality sound here at the studio.'

If that bit of cable and doodahs could do that, I wanted it! But how did it work?

He reached for the phone receiver and unscrewed the mouthpiece. 'That's the microphone,' he said, pointing to a disc-shaped object. 'That's your problem—poor-quality mic, poor-quality sound.'

He took the two bulldog clips and attached them to the wires behind the telephone mic, and plugged the jack at the other end of the cable into the output of the recorder.

'There you are—straight from the recorder onto the phone line, with no loss of quality.' He was very pleased with himself.

'Who came up with this idea?' I asked.

'Me.'

'Is it legal?'

'Who's to know?'

Who indeed? And that couple of cents worth of equipment saved hours of time—and was only one of the magic tricks those PMG technicians produced.

SHINDY'S

'THE TRACK IS LIGHTNING-FAST, AND THE ROSE GARDENS ARE JUST coming into full bloom.'

We might have been talking about Royal Randwick, but we weren't. We were on the phone to Shindy Mitchell. Every year, just before the Louth races, Shindy would ring 2CR to spruik the big event, and we'd gravely discuss the state of the famous rose gardens.

Louth has a district population of, I guess, 100 or 150. But it is one of those tiny towns that's been able to develop its once-a-year race meeting into a 'bush experience' for the punters. It's not unusual to see 4000 or 5000 turn up for the big day, and there's little chance of them trampling the rose gardens—there aren't any, but Shindy could always spin a yarn.

He was one of the great Western Division characters. The story goes that he once received a letter addressed to 'Shindy Mitchell, Australia'. I don't doubt it.

Shindy's Inn was and is something of an institution out on the Darling. A party of touring actors once stopped there for a beer on their way through to Broken Hill for an engagement. This was too good an opportunity to miss, so Shindy offered an invitation: 'Put the show on here.' They did, and they got a house.

You could always get a crowd into Shindy's—or, as it turned out, out of Shindy's.

At 2CR we once fielded a desperate appeal for help from a distraught family in Bathurst. They'd just celebrated a family wedding, and the bride and groom had left for a honeymoon fishing out on the Darling. Tragically, the bride's mother died the day after the wedding.

How to contact the honeymooning couple? We rang Shindy's and they cleared the bar, sending the patrons up and down the river to look for the couple.

THE FABULOUS FOUR

I WAS SUPPOSED TO BE THEIR TEACHER, BUT THEY WERE SO MUCH WISER than me. In a matter of weeks, they became teacher—and what gentle teachers they were.

We called it the Colombo Plan. Students from Asia and Africa would come to Australia and we would teach them. Oh yes, we would teach them. The ABC was an enthusiastic teacher. We'd show these people how to communicate with their farmers—after all, no one did this farmer education business better than Aunty.

Nanda, from Sri Lanka, in her sari with bare midriff, looked a touch uncomfortable as I met her off the plane in an Orange winter. Nuri, an Afghan woman, spoke English 'just a little'. And Lahani and Vimal, the two Nepalese men, had a worldly-wise swagger about them. All four of them were going to work with me for the next three months.

Mount Canobolas was on the way back from the airport, and there was *snow* at the summit! I decided to take them for a run up. They'd like to see that, I was sure.

It had been a modest fall, all of 6 or 7 inches. Strangely, neither Nuri nor the two men seemed impressed. Nanda's bare midriff turned an interesting shade of purple.

Nuri would live with us. Friends had agreed to take Nanda into their home. For the two men, the local pub would be home for the next three months.

Cultural sensitivity wasn't my strong point back then, and I wasn't on my own. Aunty had been known to send Hindu and

Muslim off together into the Australian bush to 'learn', and been quite surprised when near murder was committed instead. No, I didn't make any allowances for the fact that this quartet had suddenly been thrown together in a strange country with a very young man who had a high opinion of his capabilities.

Nanda was a broadcaster and English was her second language. Nuri had just graduated as an economist and spoke very little English; in a marvel of maladministration, someone had decided that this city-bred, cultured woman would be a great broadcaster of farming techniques. My Nepalese guests were chalk and cheese. Lahani was 'a poet' and the king's nephew. Vimal was a hard-boiled journalist. We were going to get on just fine.

We organised a welcome dinner. Local farmers, plus some friends of ours and Nanda's new family, were invited for a meet-and-greet at our house. Diana was doing her bit to see that things went smoothly, and was flat-out in the kitchen when Nanda informed me that she would take a bath before dinner.

'Nanda wants a bath,' I told my wife.

'Now?' Diana asked.

'Now.'

'So?'

'Well, she doesn't know how to operate the heater.'

'Tell her.'

'She's a lady. I can't go into the bathroom with a lady.'

'Oh, get out of the way.'

Nanda's English, she assured us, was very good. She broadcast in English, so communication would not be a problem.

We had a gas bath heater. You might remember the type. Turn on the gas, it heats a plate. Water runs across the plate. Instant hot water.

Diana demonstrated. 'This is the gas control. Turn it this way and the gas will ignite. This is the tap. Turn it this way and water will flow. Can you manage?'

She received a withering look in return. Lesson one: don't patronise Nanda.

There were still a couple of hours before our other guests would arrive, and I was making awkward attempts at getting a conversation going. Vimal and Lahani were chatting happily to each other, and Nuri was doing her best to understand what I was trying to say, and to show some interest.

'*Eeeyow! Ha! Ha! Haaa!*'

What a strange sound . . . It was coming from the bathroom.

'*Whaa! Whaa! Whaa! Whaa!*' A rhythmic thumping. That too was coming from the bathroom. God—it was the heater. It was going to blow up!

The screams lifted an octave, running up to a breathless crescendo. The sequence repeated—up another octave, and again a run up the cut scales—and all the time the growl of the heater deepened. Obviously, Nanda had the gas up high and hadn't yet worked out how to turn on the water.

Now there was a terrifying thumping at the bathroom door. Nanda had given up any thought of controlling this beast. She wanted out.

'Nanda, turn on the water! The water, Nanda,' I yelled. 'Diana, Nanda's having trouble with the heater.'

'So go in and turn the water on.'

'She might be in the . . . you know.'

'Oh, get out of the way. Nanda, let me in. Nanda!'

The screams had subsided, to be replaced by a despairing and repeated sob, and all the while the growl of the heater grew more menacing.

Nanda was going to get out of that bathroom no matter what happened, but in her panic (there, I've used the word) she was trying to open the door outwards. On the other side, Diana was equally determined to open the door inwards. And all the time the heater heated.

Lahani and Vimal were beginning to show interest. Would they do the gentlemanly thing and go to her assistance? Not a bit of it. This was great entertainment. Let's see what happens.

I'd joined Diana at the door.

'Give it a good shove and get her out of the way,' I was instructed.

'I might push her back onto the heater.'

'Give it a shove!'

'Yes, dear.'

Diana burst in, the door slammed shut behind her and the growl turned to a nasty, prolonged *hisss*. Instant sauna.

'Turn on the water, Nanda,' Diana said calmly. 'I showed you.'

'I know. I know.'

Diana returned to the kitchen and the awkward attempts at conversation returned, but with an edge. Everyone had an ear and an eye to the bathroom door.

It took a long time, but Nanda emerged glowing in a fresh sari.

One look from her was enough. Nothing had happened. In the unlikely event that some of us might think that she had been in distress—or, worse, had panicked—well, we were mistaken. She'd simply been left to deal with a defective machine.

Already we were learning.

SPUD LUMPING

I blame Neil Inall. He insisted that we make our interviews 'real'. None of this finding a nice quiet spot to record the interview. No, get out there where there was some background noise. Let people know that we were there on the spot. He was right, but it meant learning how to balance that background sound with the foreground sound, and sometimes things didn't go according to plan. He led the way.

Millthorpe is a small community just to the south of Orange, and the locals prided themselves on the spuds they grew and the men who lumped the bags. It was inevitable that there'd be competition as to who was the best spud lumper in the district—and just as inevitable that the question would be debated in one of the local pubs.

And so the Millthorpe Murphy Marathon was born, a race from one pub to the next with a bag of spuds on your back. Neil would cover the story.

He lined up with the starters, his Nagra tape recorder firmly strapped down and his microphone at the ready. He 'called' the race while running with the contestants. *AM*, the ABC's elite current-affairs program, bought the story. Millthorpe was on the map and we were mightily impressed. There'd be more of this.

WHO YOU KNOW

THE NEWS WAS OUT THAT A MAN ON THE RUN HAD THE DIRT ON THE infamous Roger Rogerson. The Federal Police had the fugitive in safekeeping somewhere or other, and they hoped to use him to break up a drug-smuggling ring. Supposedly, no one knew where he was.

PM, the ABC's top afternoon radio current-affairs program, got the tip that the mystery man might be somewhere in 2CR country, and asked if I could pick up any information as to his whereabouts.

Strangers stand out in small communities, especially strangers with a police escort. So it was only a matter of knowing where to ask—and, I suppose, of being trusted with the information. I was directed to our man and set off with mic and recorder.

It was an isolated farmhouse with a Federal Police officer at the front gate, who was obviously not pleased to see me. He muttered into a walkie-talkie and let me through.

Our man was very happy to talk. He really wanted to stay out of jail, for fairly obvious reasons; he had recorded telephone conversations he wanted to play for me; and he was prepared to talk for as long as I was prepared to let the tape recorder roll.

Oh, was he cooperative. Disconcertingly, he held a nasty-looking .303 rifle the whole time. I reasoned that the Federal Police were unlikely to let him anywhere near a loaded weapon. Still . . .

The producer of *PM* expressed his amazement when I booked a landline to send the story through. 'You found him?'

'Yes.'

'No one was supposed to know where he is.'

'You have to know who to ask.'

AROUND THE WEST

TV CAME TO THE CENTRAL WEST OF NEW SOUTH WALES IN 1962 AND changed the way people listened to radio. No more sitting around the set at night listening to serials or symphonies—except of course in the Far West of New South Wales. No TV there until satellite technology came along in the mid-1980s.

2CR responded to their needs with a very old-fashioned radio program just for the West. Every Wednesday night, Pat Britten would put to air *Around the West*, a program of music, news and stories especially for the people in the Western Division. It involved an extraordinary suspension of belief on the part of listeners and presenters to make it happen.

Twice a year Pat and a selection of staff from 2CR would fly out to the west and binge-collect stories to keep the program running. Two would be dropped off at, say, Cobar, and the plane would fly on to drop the other pair off at, say, Brewarrina. Then would follow the most extraordinary couple of days.

A listener would meet us at the airfield. After a brief introduction, we would be told that so-and-so has an important story 20 miles out of town. Who's covering that? Decision made.

Next stop a motel, where the other reporter would be ushered into a room where a crocodile was already forming outside the door.

Enter a young (or old) man (or woman).

'Yes? What's the story?' we would ask.

'The debutante ball (or cricket club, or race meeting).'

Then you'd get down to it. The first thing to establish would be when this event might take place. Let's say it was on a Saturday sometime in the future. You'd explain to the interviewee that Pat would be putting the story to air on the Wednesday before the event. 'So whenever you mention the ball, you say "next Saturday"—okay?' It always was.

One by one they'd come through the door, and little by little tins would fill with recorded tape, and in a month (or two months, or three months), they'd listen to themselves on air talking about the big event happening 'next Saturday'.

Looking at it like that, it was truly *Alice in Wonderland* stuff, but there was real affection for the listeners and from the listeners. Where else would you know so many of your listeners by name?

I did stories on everything from a young man's first attempt at directing (Tennessee Williams' *The Glass Menagerie* at Walgett—not a bad way to make a debut), through to a celebration cricket match at the Keragundi Cricket Club. The club's home ground was a claypan, and the story went that if you could hit the ball past a fielder it was a certain four—the ball actually picked up speed as it went.

I assisted a bush nurse with a patient. A young Aboriginal kid presented with so many burrs in his feet that he could no longer walk. I restrained him as she picked them out one at a time. It's still a vivid memory for me—and I bet for him.

And we flew into a dust storm, where we couldn't see the wing tips. We weren't worried until, after we'd landed, the pilot had a little nervous 'spit' under the wing.

Later, I got to see the Keragundi home ground. Russell Drysdale missed an opportunity – a wire-netting boundary fence with a bough-shed on a claypan. The claypan was much, much bigger than the ground, and with the sun in just the right position you could see little shadows all across it. Those shadows were cast by the remains of ancient fires. Often beside the fire was a hard-baked mud wasps' nest – an after-dinner delicacy?

They eventually set up volunteer video exchange systems in the Far West, and *Around the West* quietly died, but it was a lovely anachronism. Pat put his heart and soul into the show. There was real love and respect for the people he was talking to.

BURRUMBUTTOCK BREKKIE

I REMEMBER ONCE HAVING TO REPORT ON A MEETING IN THE LITTLE town of Burrumbuttock. Guessing that it would be a late night, I booked into the local pub.

'I won't get home before closing,' I told the publican when I arrived. 'Any chance of a key?'

My host tossed me a bunch. I had the keys to the pub.

He was feeding a poddy lamb when I poked my head out in the morning.

'Bacon and eggs sound alright for breakfast,' he asked.

'Do me,' I replied.

'There's some in the fridge,' he said. 'I'll have my eggs fried. Make it a couple.'

BLACK BEAUTY

THERE WAS MOVEMENT AT THE STATION—THE COUNTRY AND THE WAY it did business was changing. Grazing country was going under the plough at an alarming rate. Drought and flooding rains were slowly giving way to the ordered flow of irrigating water.

Crops never before seen in this part of the country, and how to grow them, were now 'the' topic in pubs, saleyards and wherever stockmen-turned-farmers met. Our listeners were hungry for information, and the traditional sources of supply couldn't keep up. There were no research results in this part of the world to form the basis of advice. We were all flying blind.

Neil Inall was developing new means to meet the demand. An agronomist turned broadcaster, he had experience and contacts in the southern New South Wales farming districts. He organised a bus trip: novice irrigators would meet old hands, farmers would teach farmers one-to-one, with a radio station the conduit. Unheard-of stuff.

We were playing with television too. We'd started showing 'our country' to city audiences by way of the cheekily titled weekly program *A Big Country*, which had started in 1968, the year after I joined the ABC. In its very early days it had no dedicated reporters; the original concept was for rural reporters to suggest a story and, if it was accepted, take on the role of reporter.

I reckoned there was a great television story waiting to be told out in the Macquarie Marshes if—and it was a big if—we could tell it. And the Deputy Director of the Rural Department, John Treffry, was coming on an orientation tour. So much was happening so quickly; the department needed to get a handle on it.

John arrived in a 'Yank tank', one of those Ford models that were all bonnet and boot. Straight out of the ABC's garage in William Street, Sydney, it gleamed black above the crimson 'C' for Commonwealth on its numberplate. The locals would certainly know we'd arrived. John could get a look at the changing country and provide the transport, while I scouted for a possible TV story in the Marshes.

The Marsh country drains the Macquarie and Talbragar rivers. When they flood, water spreads naturally through the Marsh and onto the properties around them, irrigating thousands of acres. It's home to millions of waterbirds, snakes, roos and wild pigs, which thrive in the protection of the tangled lignum scrub that grows in the Marsh. And of course it's home to some magnificent mobs of cattle.

Over the generations, stockmen had developed a system of managing this wild and beautiful country. Once a year they'd gather from the surrounding stations and muster the Marsh, bringing the cattle out and dividing them station by station. This was a mirror image of the famous High Country musters—'Man from Snowy River' stuff—but with some important differences. Here the riders faced not mountain gorges but tangles of lignum tunnelled through by pigs. It was dangerous work, and with the way things were, they'd soon be doing it for the last time.

The first of the allocated irrigation water from Burrendong Dam, specially built to tame those floods, had been released just a couple of years earlier. The Marsh was shrinking, and while new farmers were struggling to come to terms with grain sorghum as a crop, innovators were following the water and buying up country. The first white blossoms of cotton were pocking the country, and cotton is a thirsty crop. Each new paddock drained the Marsh a little more.

On Sandy Camp, one of the big stations fringing the Marsh, Mrs Moxham was already seeing the changes. She rode with the best of them at the muster and knew that its days were numbered. She told me the story on tape.

That made for good radio, but what chance did television have of covering it? I could see her on horseback bringing the stockman's craft to life for the audiences of Sydney, but the big question was: could a camera follow her and the other riders into the Marsh?

'How are you on a horse?' she asked.

My old boss, when I was a young jackeroo, was never very complimentary about my ability in that area. In his view, about the only place I was safe was 'in a spring cart with a net over it'. I was better than that, but I couldn't mix it with Marsh riders in country I'd never seen before, and we'd never get a film crew in there. We'd be a danger to ourselves—and to whoever had to nursemaid us. Regretfully, I acknowledged that this was not for television.

While I'd been getting (not getting) the Marsh story, John had been taken in hand by some of the new irrigators. I'd taken longer than expected, and when I was delivered back to town, the Yank tank— aka Black Beauty—was at rest outside the Spider's Web, Carinda's great little pub. John was being entertained by his new friends, but we were due in Walgett that night.

We'd been joined on the trip by a friend of his—a former ABC rural reporter who was now an orchardist—so we were a party of three. Dusk wasn't all that far away, and I wasn't keen on driving the 50 or so miles at night. You never knew what you'd come across on that road . . . 'Here be dragons,' as the old maps would warn.

'We could stay here,' I offered.

'What's to eat?' John demanded.

There was no counter meal. 'Ah, I could get some biscuits and cheese,' I suggested.

'Walgett,' John decided.

No bombing raid over Germany was ever more carefully briefed. 'Now, there are all sorts of things out there,' I explained. 'Pigs are the worst. If we hit one, it'll take the front end out and we'll be spending the night on the road.'

'Pigs,' John sniffed.

Everyone in the car wanted to talk at once. John was enthusing about the new cropping regime, and I was pleading for some miracle that would let us film the Marsh story. Suddenly, a black shadow that looked to be the size of a minibus almost got us.

'That was a pig!' John sounded incredulous.

'Humnh.' How do you say 'I told you so' politely?

Black Beauty cruised on towards Walgett—now in watchful, strained silence.

Incredibly, even around Walgett the talk was of cropping. Surely the country was too dry? Too unreliable? The optimists argued that one crop in three years would be a just reward if the price of the land was right, and already farming families from safe farming districts, where neighbours hemmed in any chance of expansion, were selling out and buying into country with space to burn.

Black Beauty rolled the road from Walgett to Bourke, but she was no longer pristine. Now the odd nervous rattle marked her transition from city street to dirt road, but at least we hadn't hit anything.

Nothing much had changed in the Western Division since soldier settlement broke up the big runs. Old, established families were managing the encroachment of scrub, the legacy of the changed grazing practices forced by the breakup of the big stations, and there was talk that there 'might be money in these wild goats'.

John was anxious to see the country. I had a story I could pick up near Louth, so on we rolled.

John had developed a theory. Roos were now the big risk at dusk, he concluded, but 'they always jump from right to left'. He'd been studying their pattern and was convinced that, if only the driver kept a sharp lookout to the right, the risk of collision was minimal. Well, outback travel can be boring. You need something to occupy the mind.

I don't know if it happens now, but then, when the dirt road started to break up badly, the locals would drop down to the table drain at the side of the road for smoother passage, and it was a wise driver who followed the obvious run-off. 'You learn something every day,' John observed as we cruised along looking at the rutted potholed road beside us.

Shindy Mitchell was holding court at his pub at Louth. John was thrilled; he could have a beer with a legend. Shindy was a great supporter of 2CR and was only too happy to play host.

When I loaded John back into Black Beauty sometime in the midafternoon, he was disappointed. 'Shindy drinks ponies,' he confided, referring to five-ounce glasses. An idol with feet of clay.

How to point out diplomatically that there might be a reason for that? Matching Shindy middy for pony was a dangerous game.

We'd travelled perhaps 20 of the 50 miles from Louth to Bourke. John's theory was holding water. Every roo we'd encountered jumped from right to left. He was delighted. But two is not a statistically accurate sample, John.

It was sometime after five in the afternoon when the exception to prove the rule came in from the left. He was a very big red and he made a proper job of it. He came in through the grille, removing the radiator, and wrapped that great big bonnet around the windscreen. We were going nowhere.

John scrambled from his seat in a flash. The big red was wedged in; fortunately (for us, not so for him), he was very dead so we could haul him out. John wanted an ear for a souvenir, while I contemplated a night on the Bourke Road.

Salvation took the form of a shearer heading into town. He was driving a Holden ute with room for two passengers at a squeeze.

He'd take John and our passenger into Bourke. I'd stay with Beauty and our gear, and they'd send a tow truck for me in the morning.

John got to meet a great character. Our shearer had a Coca-Cola bottle opener welded to the dashboard of the ute at his right hand. At his left hand was an unending supply of stubbies. He could pluck a stubby with his left, flip it to his right, decapitate it and despatch it while maintaining an endless string of yarns and a heart-stopping 70 miles per hour.

In Bourke they replaced Beauty's radiator. They reattached the now very mangled crimson 'C' numberplate, and reconfigured her bonnet enough for it to be secured by a piece of number 8 fencing wire. Black Beauty had failed the country road test.

The trip back to Orange was uneventful, but John's trip back to William Street was a triumphal procession. Clad in the red dust of battle, her bonnet flapping against the restraint of a bit of wire, on her arrival Black Beauty shouldered aside her city cousins. She and John had been bush. She bore the scars, and he had a roo's right ear to prove it.

CARINDA CURRY

O<small>NE BY ONE</small> I <small>INTRODUCED THE</small> F<small>ABULOUS</small> F<small>OUR TO OUR LISTENERS.</small> They read the market reports at half past six in the morning, and they practised interviewing each other and editing the results.

We discussed such lofty subjects as what might be the best time of the day to broadcast farming material. Lahani was loath to join in the discussion. When I prompted him, he offered: 'In my country everyone in a certain area is having a wireless, and when I am broadcasting they must listen.'

That's one way of boosting the ratings.

When I introduced the subject of the long-running radio serial *Blue Hills* and its predecessor, *The Lawsons*, and explained how they'd been used to promote everything from the integration of 'New Australians' to the use of superphosphate as a fertiliser, he sparked up. Drama! This was something worthy of his talents. He would listen to this program and give me his opinion.

In a very short period of time the four became part of the 2CR family. It seems silly to say it now, but two Nepalese men, a Sri Lankan woman and an Afghan woman were a novelty. Everyone wanted to meet them. They turned up at our children's school fete. Nanda in her sari created a sensation, and she and Nuri even conducted some interviews there with the kids.

Lahani had a truly beautiful voice and loved to sing. He told us it was his poetry, and he practised it at every possible occasion. Schools invited him, and he came and he sang. I looked at some old photos of them recently, and remembered with a shock that all the time Nuri was with us, she wore a hijab. No one had commented then. Wasn't that her national costume?

The time came for a field trip. I'd been stuck in the studio with them for too long. I needed to get out and collect some stories for my programs. With irrigation being the big talking point at this time, grain sorghum was the buzz crop, and small cooperatives everywhere were setting up their own irrigation schemes. I wanted to head out again to the Macquarie Marshes.

A good central point was the town of Carinda. But this wasn't going to be a get-there-and-back-in-a-day trip; we'd need a couple of days on the road. Could I get accommodation for five in town? Nuri and Nanda would need separate rooms, that much was certain. Lahani and Vimal could share, or I'd be happy to share with either of them; but we'd need at least four rooms.

No trouble. They were going to get a taste of an Aussie country pub. I made contact with the people I wanted to interview, and we mentioned, on air, that we were headed for Carinda. Within minutes, the Fab Four had an invitation to visit the local school.

Carinda wasn't a big town. We'd recently broadcast news of what had to be the ultimate embarrassment. When a fire had broken out in town, the volunteer brigade reported for duty but couldn't get the fire truck started. This hadn't stopped them attending the conflagration: they simply pushed the truck down the street to the job. Later they had the good sense to have a laugh at themselves. Carinda wasn't a big town, but it had a big heart.

We arrived to find that the local women had arranged what could only be described as a civic reception for their guests. Dressed in their best, the women packed the hall, and each had attempted to outdo her neighbours with the food she'd brought. The long table for the guests of honour looked as though it had come straight from the Best In Show line-up at the Sydney Royal. The Fab Four were going to try the best of what country cooks had to offer—with one tiny exception.

The news was out that four 'Indians' were coming to town. It would be inhospitable not to offer them a curry. There, in front of Vimal and Lahani, was a large dish. Its contents were green and grievous. I swear that if the bowl had been lined with enamel, it would have been peeling. And their hosts were pressing them: 'Eat! Eat!'

Long afterwards, they'd recount their experience. 'You've heard of vindaloo? Ha! Wait till you try Carinda Curry.'

THE GRAZIER'S NEW WIFE

IT WAS A BRAND-NEW HOMESTEAD THAT WOULD NOT HAVE BEEN OUT OF place in suburban Sydney or Melbourne. The young grazier's wife, like the house, was new, a city girl determined to make her way in her new community. Around the house's perimeter was a new lawn struggling to get a foothold.

Her husband kept reminding her that she was now in the bush. Over and over, he drummed into her that 'water is precious'. Yes, the lawn could be watered but not too much.

She'd done the morning chores. He was up the paddock somewhere and she'd set the sprinkler up on the lawn. Now for a shower.

It must have been the luxury of the shower that pricked her conscience—that sprinkler needed shifting. Clad in no more than a shower cap—well, she was miles from anywhere—she sprinted out to the lawn. She bent to retrieve the sprinkler and felt a sharp pain in her toe. A snake had been enjoying its own personal shower, and she'd been bitten.

This was a young lady straight out of Sydney. There was no way of contacting her new husband. She was miles from town and he had the only family vehicle. She can be forgiven a mild panic. Her only hope was a neighbour, an old confirmed bachelor whom she'd met only once.

There is a god—the man was at home, and he answered the phone. 'Don't panic,' he told her. 'The important thing is to keep calm. I'm on my way, and you'll be at the hospital in no time. Now, do you know what sort of snake it was?'

She couldn't be sure. She thought brown.

'A couple of things to do straight away,' he said. 'Where's the bite?'

'On my toe.'

'So, can you scarify it? Take a razor blade and—'

'No, no, I couldn't cut myself,' she protested.

'Then you'll need a tourniquet,' the old bloke told her.

'Yes, I can do that.'

'So, apply a tourniquet and relax. I'm on my way. You'll be okay. Oh, and stick your leg up on something. Keep it up in the air.'

The young lady followed his instructions to the letter. The nearest thing she could find that would make a tourniquet was the cord of a new Holland blind shading her windows, so she used that.

And that's where her saviour found her: her foot resting on the window sill, a blind cord around her toe and a shower cap on her head.

DUNLOP

Mr Murray owned Dunlop Station out on the Darling. Dunlop was the first shed in Australia to adopt machine shearing. Its shearing board was reputed to be a hundred yards long. Riverboats loaded scoured wool straight from the station's jetty for transport to the spinning mills in England. It was the Australian wool industry in a time capsule, and Mr Murray held the keys.

Yes, he said, he would be pleased to welcome me. I couldn't get out to Louth and across the river quickly enough.

It would be very wrong to describe Mr Murray as 'patrician'. That term conjures up images of strong aquiline noses, for looking down—but in country where the 'characters' are big, loud and larger than life, he stood apart. He was quiet, reserved and, in the truest sense, a gentleman. He had a calmness about him that said, 'I know who I am and I'm comfortable with that.' He called me 'Mr Nicol' and we had tea.

In the 1960s, Dunlop Homestead was cool, dark and substantial, but its glory days were a hundred years behind it. Mr Murray showed me old photographs, from a time when the staff had been numerous enough to populate a small town. They were grouped around an ornamental lake in front of the house. The manager and his lady reclined in a punt. On the banks, employees were carefully grouped according to rank. They were all there, right down to the local Aboriginal 'king', complete with brass breastplate, and the Chinese cook and gardeners. For the record, the 'king' had precedence over the Chinese cook and gardeners.

Records were presented next. Details of thousands of rams— that's right, thousands of rams—joined the flock in one season.

He wanted to show me the plans of the elaborate irrigation system that a hundred years earlier took water from the river and used gravity to irrigate the acres needed to grow the feed, to make the chaff, to feed the hundreds of horses that worked the place.

And he had a collection of curios he'd found. He weighed a stone axe in his hand and mused sadly about the size and strength of the man who'd used that, compared with the Aborigines around these days. There was a small, square bottle blued from years of exposure to the sun. 'It's an opium bottle. Opium used to be part of the wages—like tobacco, you know.'

I ventured that it must have been tremendously isolated at that time.

'For the old people, for the children,' he said, and talked about the coach and train trip needed to get to and from school in Bathurst.

I had the tape recorder loaded and ready to go, so I put it on the table between us and suggested that I'd like to get some of his memories on tape.

'Oh, I'd rather not, Mr Nicol. I've heard people talk on the radio before and they've been critical of those who've come before. I don't think that's right.'

He talked about the 'old people', those who'd lived and worked on Dunlop all those years ago, as if they were still about the place somewhere and could hear what he said. It would be disrespectful to talk about them when they couldn't defend themselves. My pleas were in vain.

'Would you like to see the shed?' He led me through what really were the remains of a small town. 'Most of the staff went to the First World War, and then, of course, we had soldier settlement.'

That obviously pained the old man. Not because it meant the breaking up of an iconic property, but because it changed forever the way the country was managed—and, he feared, changed it for the worse.

Uniquely, some of Dunlop was freehold country, and that was sacrosanct, but much of the station was leasehold and so was broken up for soldier settlement after the war. Mr Murray lamented the resultant separation of black-soil country from red-soil country. 'It completely changed the system of management, which had been to stock the black country in the good seasons, rest it in the tough times, and take advantage of the feed that showers will bring on the lighter red soil.'

He blamed the breakup for the degradation of the country, the increase in scrub. The country no longer had the chance to rest; ironically, though there were now more properties, there was fewer stock.

He stopped at a jumble of rough wooden frames. 'Pack-saddles for camels,' he told me.

'They don't look too comfortable,' I said.

'Oh, the poor brutes suffered. They decided on the standard size of a bale of wool as the load that a camel could carry, you know. Bull camels would carry the bales of locks. Goodness knows how much some of those weighed. They used to say that so long as a camel could stand up with the load, he could carry it. Sometimes they'd heat up great branding irons and brand the camel until he lurched to his feet—very cruel. Sometimes the drivers would come onto Dunlop with camels rubbed red-raw by those pack-saddles—big open wounds. They'd beg green sheepskins and stitch a piece into the wound.'

'Ha, early skin grafts,' I said.

'I suppose you could say that.' Cruelty to animals was obviously something that didn't sit well with Mr Murray.

It's difficult to describe what I saw in the Dunlop shed. Everything said, 'Look at me. I have been glorious.' The board really was a

Dunlop on the Darling in 1886—a time capsule of the wool industry.

hundred yards long. God, the men who must have shorn there. Jackie Howe, the Bradman of shearers—did Jackie Howe shear here? Which was his stand?

There was room to shear thousands of sheep under cover. The wool bins weren't bins; they were chutes that dropped the wool straight down into waiting drays to be carted to the scour. Looking down the chutes, you could see the rub marks made by the wheel hubs on the uprights. All the wood was polished with the years of wool grease it had absorbed.

I wondered what this place would have been like during shearing. A hundred shearers. There must have been close to a thousand people employed in and around this shed. Wool production on an industrial scale.

And look at it now. The corrugated iron was as thin as an old man's skin. Years of abrasive western winds were wearing it away.

THEY'RE RACING

THERE'S A HISTORY OF HORSERACING IN MY FAMILY. GREAT UNCLE HERB stood as a bookmaker on the Flat in Sydney—and ran an SP business on the side. My father was a professional punter at the age of fourteen.

My grandparents were concerned that their only son hadn't brought a report card home. A query to the good Marist Brothers brought the response that you couldn't report on someone who hadn't been to school. Dad was getting his education at the track. If you asked him how much you stood to win with five bob on a nag that came home at 6/4, he could do that in a flash.

My grandfather took Dad by the ear and apprenticed him (apparently you could then) as a grocer at Mark Foy's. He brought his pay packet home every week. Well, every week until he had a run of bad luck.

The track had a terrible fascination for him. He told us kids how you could go from being flat broke to getting a stake to go to the races.

First, you get some 'store money'. Before the days of credit cards and hire purchase, the big retailers would issue 'store money'—a token you could spend in that store and nowhere else. Then you use this store credit to buy a couple of nice shirts. Take the shirts across the road, still in their wrapping, to 'uncle' at the pawnshop. Pop the shirts for half their value, and there you are—you're off to the races. If you got very lucky, you could pay for the store money and get the shirts back.

A family story goes that the cops raided Uncle Herb's SP business one day. Granny, a very gentle Irish lass, grabbed the betting slips and popped them into the gozunder—the chamber pot—and then slipped her knickers down and sat on them. It would be a very brave constable who'd disturb a lady in that situation.

Time was when you got three classes at the races. Put up your money and you got into the Paddock; down a step, you'd queue to get into the Ledger. The Flat was for the hoi polloi, and that was where Uncle Herb called the odds. He used tell the tale of a regular customer who'd use her wedding ring for collateral for a sixpenny bet in the last race. If luck was with her, she'd be back for the winnings; if not, she'd turn up on Tuesday with sixpence to redeem the ring. It was that sort of a place.

Herb was around when they ran pony races in Sydney. The ponies ran in divisions depending on their height—14.1 or 14.2 hands. They were an anathema to the establishment, and inspired some imaginative schemes. Herb told of trainers rasping hooves down to make the height divisions, and he'd laugh till the tears ran down his face as he described one of the last races held for the tiny horses.

It was a two-horse race, and neither wanted to win. That's putting it mildly. Let's say neither could afford to win. The further the race went, the more obvious that became, and the more desperate the jockeys. Halfway down the straight, with the punters venting their disapproval, one jockey slipped from the saddle and crashed to the track. That should do it.

Left in front and with the winning post looming, his companion did the only possible thing. He pulled up, dismounted and went to render aid to his fallen comrade.

Life for both, and a police escort to safety.

A PARTING GIFT

No one wanted the Fab Four to go, but time was up. They decided that they'd like to host a dinner party for the people who'd been so kind to them. They'd do the cooking. Nanda and Nuri presented Diana with a list of ingredients, and she scoured town in an attempt to find them. An Italian friend came to the rescue, opening her cupboard. 'You'll never get any of that in town,' she said.

Nanda, of course, would cook a curry. Nuri offered chicken stuffed with fruits and baked inside a coating of rice. The men would cook too—they'd produce their national dish, dhal.

Nanda cooked at her host family's house. Nuri worked away in our kitchen, and the men got in the way. Anything and everything went into their dish and, as with the sorcerer's apprentice, things rapidly got out of control. Thank the lord Diana had a large jam pot, because we were going to have plenty of dhal left over. Their contribution complete the men returned to the pub to 'dress' for dinner.

It snowed quite heavily the night of the farewell. Nanda was brilliant in her sari, and her curry was unlike anything I'd ever tasted. Nuri's chicken was beautiful, despite her protestations that it should have been cooked in a clay oven. The dhal was indescribable.

The party was in full swing, but the men were absent. I'd forgotten. It was snowing. I should be at the pub to pick them up.

Then they swanned into the room. They'd walked four or five blocks through the snow, and for the first time they were dressed in what might pass as their national costume – snow-white tight trousers, a little white jacket and a black cap.

'I'm so sorry,' I said. 'I should have been at the pub to pick you up. You must be frozen.'

A patronising smile, and in unison they opened the front of those little white jackets to reveal a ribbed kapok-filled undershirt. Look and learn, boss cocky.

There were speeches, of course, and gifts. Vimal and Lahani's gift was unusual. 'Tell me, Alex, how long is it you can make the sex act last?' they asked.

I had to confess that I'd never timed myself.

'We are giving you some pills that will make you last at least half an hour.' They were beside themselves.

'Please, don't bother,' offered Diana.

There were real tears and hugs next day at the airport.

The next year I was summoned to Sydney to give the introductory remarks to a new intake of Colombo Plan students. We had learned, and no longer did we throw groups together willy-nilly. Now students were encouraged to choose their partners for the bush trip.

At cup-of-tea-and-a-chat time, I was approached by one of the smallest men I've ever seen. He was about five feet four but looked to be no wider than a foot across the shoulders. In Australian parlance, he would have been five stone four wringing wet.

'You are Mr Nicol?'

'I am indeed.'

'Mr Vimal and Mr Lahani are asking me to ask you if you are remembering them?'

'I do—very well indeed.'

'They are asking me to give you this gift.' He handed over a small bottle of pills.

The *Kama Sutra* with a 'best by' date. Some people never give up.

'Have you been told where you're going for the next three months?' I asked.

'I am going to Wagga Wagga. Are you knowing Wagga Wagga?'

'I know Wagga Wagga very well. And have you decided who is going with you?'

He beamed and turned to introduce me. 'These three fine ladies are looking after me.'

Behind him were three huge African women wearing beatific grins.

WATER WAR

A HEATED LOCAL CONTROVERSY IS THE MOST DIFFICULT THING LOCAL media outlets have to deal with. It's simple if the challenge comes from outside the community—you're expected to back the locals. But what happens when the community is divided against itself?

Three times during my stay at 2CR the station dealt with serious issues that divided the community. In the most serious case, the way the community reacted spoke volumes about how the bush had changed.

Don't let anyone tell you that farmers are conservative. Farming is a high-risk business, and the best farmers are among the most innovative businesspeople I know. When markets turned against the traditional grazing industries in the 1960s and '70s, those innovators were quick to see the potential value of irrigation in previously dry country. Suddenly there was considerable interest in the water available from the Macquarie River and, more importantly, from the skein of creeks and off-takes of the river that netted the country around Warren and Gulargambone.

Burrendong Dam on the Macquarie was a fact of life, but long before irrigation water from the dam had been allocated, groups of farmers began cooperatives to set up mini irrigation areas down-stream. In many cases, considerable amounts of private capital were invested to construct weirs and earthworks; some of these sparked disagreements between neighbours over whether the crop or the stock had the right to the water. On more than one occasion, mysterious night-time explosions destroyed a carefully constructed earthwork.

At the radio station, those of us reporting the development were scrambling to keep up with geography as the rights and wrongs of water flow from such mysterious places as the Marebone Break were debated. Those geography lessons landed me in a row with the New South Wales Minister for Environmental Control.

An irrigators' delegation gathered in Dubbo to hear the minister outline how water from Burrendong would be allocated. I was nearing the end of my training period at Orange, and was trusted to report on what really was a fairly complicated business.

The press was barred from the minister's meeting with the irrigators. He'd address us after he'd spoken with them. I couldn't claim to be an expert, but by then I had at least a working knowledge of the byways and waterways that would be involved. From the irrigators I collected a detailed account of what had been promised.

The press conference was a much simpler affair. I asked some questions and the minister's answers seemed to be at odds with what the irrigators had just told me. I pressed, but the press conference was wound up. The next morning, when I put my interview with the minister and with the irrigators to air, the differences were obvious.

Within an hour, Graham White, the director of the ABC's Rural Department, was on the phone. The minister was not happy. He was demanding that I be dismissed. Graham wanted the offending interviews on his desk, now.

Graham supported me. As far as he was concerned, I'd filed an accurate report—but there was a cost. The minister was demanding that, at the very least, I should be disciplined and moved.

'You're due for a move to your own region, and I was about to move you,' Graham told me. 'You understand that can't happen now. No reflection on you. The minister has told me that he'll never speak to the ABC again. I've told him that's unfortunate because there'll come a time when he'll need the ABC.'

I stayed in Orange.

SLEEPER CUTTERS

My memory says it was a horse and cart. Common sense argues that this was the 1960s, and people didn't go to work on horses and carts anymore. I'm sticking with memory.

He was a little man. He had wanted to be a jockey, but his parents were strict Presbyterians—no chance. So here he was cutting sleepers for a living. He should have been a clown or an aerialist or a lion tamer or something, because the circus was in town and I'd been sent to line up a story on it.

'The circus,' I reported back, 'is very small-time, and there is no story.'

The response from head office was something like: 'The camera crew will be there tomorrow.'

The town was Mendooran, on the edge of the Pilliga Scrub, and the local industry depended on the ironbarks that grew there. So now we'd be doing a story on sleeper cutters, and I'd found this marvellous old man as the peg for the story.

We could have slipped back 50 or 60 years. We filmed as he loaded axes, hammer and wedges into the cart. There had to be more to this business than that. It was a relief to see a modern chainsaw, neat in its case, follow them.

All in the camera and all set for the trip to the scrub and ironbarks. Then the old man turned to kiss his wife goodbye. It wasn't staged for the camera. It was obviously something the old couple did every morning, a moment of tenderness that said: 'I know where you are going is dangerous. Take care and come home safe tonight.'

The director hadn't anticipated this. 'You don't have to kiss him for the camera,' he told the wife.

'I kiss him goodbye every morning.'

Everything had to come out of the cart, and the scene was shot again. The kiss was just as gentle, just as real.

The Pilliga looked then, I guess, as it had looked for centuries. It was quiet and hot. We could have been the first people ever to venture into this little patch in search of a tree suitable to turn into squares and round backs, but a castor oil bottle opalised by years in the sun suggested that we were only the latest in a long, long line.

The old man was neat, methodical and patient. He would walk to what looked to me like an obvious tree and stand studying it. If he liked what he saw, he'd raise his axe over his head and tap the tree over and over again with the back of the axe. No. A steady walk to another black barked giant and the procedure would be repeated.

I sensed our director's growing frustration. 'We're supposed to be making a show for the mums and dads in Sydney. This is television—energy, colour, excitement.' He wanted to see the chips fly and to record a giant tree crashing to the ground, but we were watching a master practise a craft that in every way was the opposite to the director's craft. The longer I watched the old man at work, the more I learned that you didn't need straining muscles to turn a tree into timber. We set up for a chat.

He explained that, when he looked at a tree, he was measuring it. How many squares, how many round backs. These, he explained, were second-grade sleepers, cut from the outer edge of the tree. It took time to get a tree down, to clean it up, to bark it. What he was looking for was value for energy expended.

And what was that *tap, tap, tap* with the axe?

'There's a pipe in this one. The centre of the tree has rotted. Hear it?'

I couldn't. And that was why I wouldn't make a sleeper cutter.

Eventually, we watched as he felled a tree, neatly, exactly where he said it would come down. And we watched as he bruised the bark free and began to measure out his sleepers. He put a chalk line down, drove the first wedge in. 'Some people cut them out with a saw, but sleepers last longer if you split the timber along the natural grain.'

And gradually, what had been a tree was reduced to sleepers.

All the while we chatted. He told of accidents in the scrub, of old cutters and their methods. Of the days when a sleeper was finished with an adze—the broad, razor-sharp axe with a horizontal, rather than vertical, blade. 'You stand over the sleeper and swing the adze between your legs,' he explained. 'It's a bit like finishing the job with a plane.' He had an adze at home. 'Remind me to show it to you.'

He remembered one old bloke who always finished a sleeper by rubbing it down with his hat. 'In case there were any splinters. Smooth as a dance floor,' he chuckled. And all the time he worked.

I offered to knock some bark off while he was busy splitting a log he'd already cut free.

'If you like.'

Was I feeling guilty watching an old man work while I stood idle? Did I just want to speed things up a bit, so we could move on to the next bit of the story? I don't recall, but I sweated and worked twice, three times as hard as the old man for less than half the result.

By the end of the day there was a small pile of sleepers. I asked how much he'd get for them. I can't remember the answer, but I know it seemed like a lot of work for little reward.

Then we left them where they lay. He explained that, when there were enough, they'd be carted to the railway yard where, once a month, a railway man would inspect them and buy them.

'Aren't you worried that someone else could pick up your sleepers?'

He seemed genuinely surprised by the question. 'No, everybody knows these are mine.'

We'd spent the day watching a craftsman using tools that, except for the chainsaw, hadn't changed since the first sleeper slipped from an ironbark

Not everyone treated sleeper cutting as a craft. A young man with a family to support certainly cut his sleepers free with a saw. I asked him what the dimensions of a sleeper were and he rattled off length, breadth and width. I hadn't seen him measure anything and was halfway through asking how he knew that what he'd just cut was—but he cut me off: 'You want to measure it?'

He'd cut a lot of sleepers and other things besides. He'd begun making furniture from the ironbarks. Not rough-and-ready bush furniture, but some lovely quality pieces. He had two children at boarding school to support.

Mendooran's backyards and spare lots had colour in spades. Blokes in blue singlets being very public sleeper cutters for the film crew in town, all willing and wanting to spin yarns and exhibit scars.

One offered a toothless grin to our camera as he peeled off his singlet and turned to display a truly horrible scar down the length of his back. 'Got a bit pissed and backed into me Hargan.'

His 'Hargan' was a notoriously dangerous unguarded portable circular saw, a tool also known throughout the bush as 'The Widow Maker'. He'd come within millimetres of tearing out his spinal column.

Each timber cutter was a contractor to NSW Railways; a sleeper wasn't a sleeper until the bloke from the railways said so. Each cutter had his space in the Mendooran railway yard, and in every space grew a pyramid of sleepers, squares and round backs. Once a month the inspector turned up and bought them. We'd struck it lucky—tomorrow was inspection and payday.

But first those piles had to be inspected.

The process came straight out of a Victorian novel. Two men, one on either end of the sleeper, would pick it up and turn it for the inspector's scrutiny. If he liked what he saw, he struck it with a hammer, leaving a NSW Railways imprint. It was now a sleeper. It belonged to the railway.

And the men who picked up and turned hundreds of sleepers? They were paid by their fellow cutters. The going rate was two cents a sleeper.

Payment was made at the pub. Here was our director's chance for local colour. We would set up in the bar and chat to the cutters as they celebrated payday with a beer.

The cutters formed a patient line on the footpath outside the pub. Wives and kids joined the throng—they had a particular interest.

A name was called. The cutter walked into a small room, picked up his payment in cash, signed for it and immediately crossed the hallway into the bar. As the line on the footpath shrank, the noise in the bar grew—a hard, solid noise.

On the street there was another sound, sharp and singular: wives calling to husbands, conscious of the housekeeping money slipping across the bar. The sound inside grew, and outside a woman would flip a bar door open and call. Then she'd scurry to the next street door, flip it open, peer inside and call again.

We'd set up lights in the bar and they added to the heat. The idea was to single out cutters, grab a yarn, a story, a funny story—'colour'.

I tried. But nothing made sense. I'd shout—literally shout—and grin at potential storytellers, and get an unintelligible shout in reply. I jammed the sound recordist's headphones on. It made no difference. I just couldn't hear anything that the bloke on the other end of my microphone was saying. It wouldn't have mattered if I could; the sound quality would be terrible. All this 'colour' was going to waste.

And then came the party trick.

We'd seen this bloke before. He was big and he was loud and he promised salvation. He announced that he would stand on his head and drink a schooner upside down. At last—colour!

The beer was poured. He climbed onto the bar. The camera rolled. He stood on his head. He was going to pick up the glass with his teeth.

I positioned the mic right beside the glass, and asked a short question: 'What do you think of these young cutters?'

'Fucken useless.'

Then he toppled sideways, his boots crashing onto my head. The pair of us slipped ignominiously down among the boots and the bumpers.

TINY'S DEAD!

THERE WAS A BIT OF A SEA RUNNING. NOTHING TO WORRY ABOUT, BUT enough to be careful of. It was coming on dusk, and Tiny and his three mates were looking forward to a beer. They'd sink a few as soon as they got this net sorted, and whatever they'd caught boxed. Two of the quartet were already on the beach; a third was up to his knees in the surf. Tiny was up to his chest in the sea.

They were in a hurry to get finished before dark, when Tiny, as he later told me, 'committed the cardinal sin'. He turned his back on the sea.

His mates saw it coming and shouted a warning. Tiny didn't hear it, and couldn't have done much about it even if he had. A wave picked up the boat and hurled it shoreward. Tiny was in the way. The boat crashed onto his head and neck with terrible force, and then bobbed away in the backwash.

There was a scramble to get Tiny to the beach, where—in police parlance—he was 'unresponsive'. His mates worked on him frantically.

Forget it. He'd been hit in the back of a head by a boat—his boat, their boat. There was blood everywhere. He was dead.

Shock started to replace panic. No mobile phones then. No instant response. They were alone on a deserted beach. A boat and a net had to be attended to before they both became a menace, and the men had a mate cold and unmoving on the sand.

'Check him again.'

Nothing.

'Get on with making the boat safe.'

Tiny's missus—someone would have to tell her. Tiny's missus was tiny, with a tongue that could blister fresh paint. They could see it now—she'd turn on the messenger, flay him and then collapse.

Tiny was much loved. This would be terrible. Please God they were wrong about Tiny. They checked him again; nothing.

They thought about loading their mate in with the fish. Well, they thought they did. The truth was they were in shock and weren't thinking about anything very clearly. They headed back into town, to spread the word and face Tiny's missus.

Dutch courage at the pub. The publican on the phone to the authorities to report the tragedy, and 'Poor bloody Tiny' drinks all around the bar. Then the realisation: 'We shouldn't have left him.'

Back to the beach and a terrible sight. Tiny's body was gone. They of all people should have reckoned on the tide. Now his body was gone, sucked out to sea, and it was dark. They'd never find it.

They could have wept. They did. Tomorrow, first thing, every boat in the area would have to be out looking. They headed back to town to spread the alarm.

The pub was buzzing when they got back. Tiny was sitting in the corner, nursing a drink.

The publican had been a bit surprised when the big man had wandered in, wet and cold and a bit dazed, and ordered a Bonox and rum.

'Some mates of yours were in a while ago. Something about you being dead?' the publican offered as he reached for the phone to put things right.

Tiny admitted to a terrible headache. But it was the gash to the back of his head and the blood that persuaded him to take their advice that perhaps he'd better go to the hospital and get checked out.

The X-ray revealed a broken neck.

Tiny had 'come to' on the beach, and cursed his mates for deserting him. He'd staggered to his feet and walked into town and to the pub. He had a couple at the pub before they loaded him into a car for that trip to the hospital.

All that time, his big head, with a terrible gash down the back, was perched on top of a broken neck. A sneeze would have done for him.

'Lucky, eh?' Tiny grinned as he told me about it.

POONCARIE STOPOVER

I HADN'T GOT OFF TO A GOOD START IN POONCARIE. I BOOKED THE FILM crew into the local pub without, as they say, doing due diligence. The first words our host greeted us with were: 'Which one of you blokes will be doing the cooking?'

That was a bridge we'd have to cross when we got to it.

These days Pooncarie is promoted as 'a charming hamlet' on the Western Tourist Trail, and the pub boasts meals seven days a week. It has four units with en suites and there's even air conditioning. Tourism has a lot to answer for; booking into a bush pub used to be more of an adventure.

Our 'rooms' turned out to be in the backyard of the pub. They were small individual buildings that looked a lot like the meat houses you'd see on a big property: corrugated iron up to waist height, and flywire from there to the roof.

Please God there wouldn't be a dust storm.

There were two single beds in each room and no electric light. By the time the sound recordist and the cameraman loaded their gear in, things were a bit tight. At least we'd get an early night. It would be a big day tomorrow.

The dog didn't begin to bark until they turned off the generator. I suppose up till then the noise had kept him company. Now he wouldn't shut up. Part of my duties as a jackeroo had been to shut the dogs up at night, and I wished now I had the stockwhip I'd used then. One crack of the whip usually ensured silence in the camp.

I groped my way through the pitch dark. If I could find the beast and shake him by the scruff of his neck, that might do it.

Of course he was kennelled in a 44-gallon drum, and of course I kicked it. He was a friendly dog, and I think all he needed to know was that somebody or something was out there. He settled down.

DRIVING WITH MISS MURIEL

2CR BROADCAST AN ARTS PROGRAM EACH WEEK, AND ITS PRESENTER WAS Muriel Steinbeck. That name probably doesn't mean much now, but let's just say it was like having a retired Cate Blanchett in the studio. Muriel was special.

Muriel was one of our first movie stars. She starred with people like Peter Finch, and she was a pioneer in Australian television drama in an age in which it was broadcast live. She was the regular star attraction of the Lux Radio Theatre in those years when we sat around the wireless and listened to theatre.

By the mid-1960s Muriel had retired to Orange, and gave her time freely to promote the arts in the area.

She was a beautiful woman who often said that no woman should live past 60; she hated the thought of 'losing her looks'. She needn't have worried. Muriel was one of those women who turn a beautiful youth into a handsome older age. She dressed impeccably in the fashion of perhaps twenty years earlier, and never looked anything but glamorous.

Never condescending, she was tireless in encouraging the young people who'd come to be interviewed by Miss Steinbeck about their impending venture into theatre, music or whatever.

Muriel had star quality and she kept it in her retirement. She could make you think that you were terribly clever and witty. She was one of those people who, when they want to make a point in conversation, touch you. She would take your hand and hold it or, if she were sitting opposite you, to make a point during an interview, she'd reach across, looking you in the eye, and put her hand on your knee. She was completely unconscious of the effect this had, but she did it to me on a number of occasions. Trust me, it made concentrating a wee bit difficult.

Muriel was proud of the fact that she was born in Broken Hill, and perhaps it was the isolation that left her with a charming deficiency. I'd only just arrived at 2CR and was introduced to her. She'd just finished her show, and asked if we could call a taxi to take her home.

'Miss Steinbeck, I have a car outside. Could I drive you?' I asked.

'Thank you, darling.'

I was going to have Miss Steinbeck in my car! I opened the door for her and saw her comfortably settled. I started the engine, and then queried: 'Which way, Miss Steinbeck?'

'Darling, I have no idea.'

Muriel had no sense of direction at all. Even in a place like Orange, she had to rely on the kindness of strangers to get her home.

SOMEONE MUST CARE

We were out on the Darling River making a film about the dark days of drought and depression. Things were bad, very bad, and our film's title pleaded *Someone Must Care*. I will never forget two of the families we filmed on that trip. Each was doing it tougher than you could imagine, and each for a different reason.

She was what was known locally as an 'Adelady'. When there were children to be educated, it was not unusual in this part of the world for their mother to take them to Adelaide and set up residence there while they were at school. Dad would stay up bush and work the place, and the family would get together for school holidays.

In this case, Dad had died. It was the middle of a drought: wool prices were disastrously low and there were death duties to be paid and the family had land but no money. The only way to do that was to sell up in a buyer's market. Mother had come home and brought her teenage daughter with her. Neither had any experience of working a property, but they were trying to make a go of it until a buyer could be found.

We said we'd do their interview in the sheep yards, filming mother and daughter at work. However, first we needed to get the sheep in. We did a quick mustering job with the camera car on the closest mob, but as we were pushing them into the yards, I could see that the flies had been well and truly busy. They were in a bad way.

The director and I had a quick briefing. He started work shooting the two women drafting, pushing sheep about, the sort of cutaway action he'd need for the film. I started work on the sheep with a pair of dagging shears and fly dressing we found in the shed. It was a long day.

I've always had the greatest of admiration for the women who've partnered their husbands on the family farm, and I've seen the impact that tough times have had on some. I remember one who'd become obsessed with the weather forecast. She knew the times that ABC regional stations would broadcast their forecasts, and she'd turn from station to station, from South Australia across to the east, praying for the first sign of a break.

Here, we had a cultured lady who'd never worked on the land and who'd been living a relatively comfortable life in Adelaide. She and her daughter were way out of their depth. Their interviews showed two people helpless in a storm of circumstances. Not even the little things were working.

The place needed water pumped up from the Darling for stock and domestic water, and one of the locals was charging her $10 a week to come and start the pump. Before we left, she at least knew how to prime a pump.

The other place was away from the river—so far away that we'd had to abandon the luxury of the pub and camp out. It was a rough block and the prolonged drought showed just how hard this country could be. Windmills provided the stock water but, as I remember it, one of them was out of action. That meant part of the block was out of action and any feed there was useless. Dad was working to get the mill going, and that left the boy to do the stock work. He was about ten or eleven.

Here was a family on the edge. They were hanging on, but just. An older brother was away in a hostel so that he could attend school. Mum was teaching his young sibling by correspondence, and she and Dad grieved that he was not getting the same chance as his brother.

He was a solemn little boy. We filmed his mother teaching him in their home, a larger version of the meat-safe rooms we'd been enjoying at the pub. Watching him struggle through the reading lessons was a truly surreal experience—half an hour earlier, he'd showed us how to cannibalise an old mustering bike for the part he needed to keep his own bike going. An old head on young shoulders.

Dad shot roos at night, selling them to the meatworks. We'd been out with him, and even here things were tight: one shot, one roo—and always the biggest in the mob. We didn't see him miss once, and the brass was carefully collected after every shot. He reloaded every shell.

We finished filming for the day and were mucking about, waiting for our evening meal to cook. We'd camped just a little way away from the homestead and were playing French cricket: four grown men with a stick and a ball made of rolled-up sticky tape. Four of us fooling around and shouting over nothing.

I got the feeling we were being watched. Sure enough, up the hill a bit was a mill beside the house, and the little boy had climbed halfway up the mill and was watching us solemnly. It struck me that he had no idea what we were doing.

TROUBLES AT THE
CHOOK HOUSE

A VERY WELL KNOWN IDENTITY FROM THE WESTERN DISTRICT OF Victoria was president of the local race club. The annual meeting was coming up and the track needed some TLC. They'd let things slide, and so, at the last committee meeting before race day, he gave all and sundry a monumental 'pull through'.

'There'll be a working bee next weekend,' he began. 'We start at seven-thirty Saturday morning, and I'll accept no excuses. You'll all be there, and you'll be there on the dot.'

All committee members managed to present themselves at the agreed time, but their president was absent. When his car arrived sometime after smoko, it attracted a crowd.

'Where have you been? It'd better be good.'

It was.

'There's been a fox getting at me chooks night after night, and I'd just about had enough of him. I've had the shotgun propped up against the back door, expecting him to come back, and last night the dog camp goes up and there's hell to pay in the chookyard. He's back again.

'I hop out of bed, grab the gun and me torch, and race down to the chook pen. I'm crouched over inside, bent double. I've got both barrels cocked, looking for the bastard, and I see something move in the corner of the shed. I swing the light and the gun around, and as I did, Ben, our old labrador, stuck his warm, wet nose on me bare arse.

'I've been plucking fucken chooks—what do you think I've been doing?'

ALL WAYS ON SUNDAY

IT WAS NEIL INALL'S BRAINCHILD. *THIS DAY TONIGHT*, THE GROUND-breaking television current-affairs program, was just over a year old, and Neil, champion as always of rural Australia, was concerned that 'the bush isn't getting any coverage'. The ABC's Rural Department 'owned' a half-hour segment in the mishmash of programs that made up Sunday morning programming on the third network, the programs serving regional Australia. Nothing much had ever been done with this spot. It was filled on a haphazard basis with whatever 'colour' stories might be available. Neil's scheme was to use this half-hour for current-affairs material generated by rural reporters, serving the regions all around Australia. It was a brave idea.

I was his trainee, and we discussed the scheme. We decided to put a pilot program together and get a reaction from head office. We didn't call on any other rural reporters, but scoured the extensive 2CR region for the sort of stories we imagined the new program might carry. As I remember it, we had three or four 'newsy' interviews, tightly edited after the style of the radio current-affairs program *AM*, and a nice human-interest story. We still didn't have a name for the show, but the pilot went off to Sydney for a reaction.

Graham White was enthusiastic, and much more adventurous than we'd been. 'Sunday morning radio in the regions is without any coherent form,' he argued. 'Let's take it over and program from 6.30 a.m. to 10 a.m., and broadcast right across the national regional network.'

That was big-picture thinking. The name for our new program was debated, and *All Ways on Sunday*—to denote the idea of distance and travel—was decided. Certainly not *Always on Sunday*—there was no guarantee that the show would last any time at all.

In retrospect, it's surprising that senior management gave the project their approval. The Rural Department was known inside Aunty as 'the rural mafia', and this surely was a bold attempt to boost its fiefdom. But *All Ways on Sunday* was blessed from on high, and its broadcast date set.

Now there was the nuts-and-bolts business of organising reporters, selecting a producer, and deciding, most importantly, who would present the program. That someone must have a profile and be able to meld the combination of light entertainment and serious reporting envisaged for the program. But that was for someone else to worry about. Neil and I returned to Orange, our job done.

The Rural Department had a stable of reporters stationed in every region across the country. They were specialists. They knew the ins and outs of the farming industries operating in their regions. They were skilled in the business of interviewing, but none of them—none of us—had any skills in producing or presenting what would, in effect, be a light entertainment program. Specialist skills would need to be brought in. A high-profile presenter was duly recruited and contracted to host *All Ways on Sunday*.

In Orange, Neil and I were hard at work looking for the stories from our region that would air in the first program. Some two weeks before it was to go to air, Graham rang me with the news that the selected presenter had resigned, and I would be producing and presenting *All Ways on Sunday*. I thought I was terrified then, but I had no idea of what terror meant.

Thinking back, my guess is that the Chosen One took one look at the resources he would have for the program and decided it just wouldn't work. The material for the program would have to come from the nation's rural reporters. They already had full-time jobs, and any contribution they made would probably be an afterthought. There was a budget to pay freelance contributors—from memory, $30 a week, which was enough at the time to buy three contributed stories for each program. But where was the network of freelance reporters in regional Australia? And who would pull this network together? Who would produce the show?

It would be very wrong to describe *All Ways on Sunday* as a one-man show. At its heart were the talents of rural reporters scattered all over the country—without them and their input, there would have been no program—but in the studio whoever presented the program would be working alone and with minimal resources. They would be the producer, the editor, the scriptwriter and the presenter, and they'd have a store of perhaps a dozen seven-inch cans of recording tape. These would need to be recycled week after week. I suspect no one at that stage had any idea of the value of the material that the program would collect.

The program would be broadcast from Sydney. I arrived and took up what proved to be quasi-permanent residence in a Kings Cross hotel, in order to be as close as possible to the ABC studios. I'd only seen those studios briefly, during my initial employment interview and during a short formal training session. I'd sat in and watched *The Country Hour* go to air. So that's how a big studio operates . . .

Music would make up about 65 per cent of the program. I knew nothing about music. 'That will be programmed for you,' I was told. I asked by whom, and was told that some nameless women in the record library would do the job. In just about the smartest thing I've ever done, I asked if I could meet them and perhaps publicly acknowledge them during the program. They were delighted and took me to their hearts. I owe them. But I had never put a record to air and had no idea of how to 'cue' a piece of music—an art to be mastered.

The rural reporters rose to the occasion magnificently. Stories came in from all over the country. I would have some choice material for the first program, so I got down to something I knew something about: editing and scripting.

I was whisked away to be professionally photographed—in Hyde Park, which was the most 'rural' setting the photographer could find. The ABC's Publicity Department set about getting me known all over the country. A feeling of inevitability settled on me. This thing was really going to happen.

In its simplest form, a radio program is a gigantic mental arithmetic problem. It will start at a precise time and it will terminate at a precise time. In between, there will be news broadcasts. They will begin at precise times and conclude less precisely. Your problem for today is to take all your scripted pieces, and all the interviews you plan to use, and all the pieces of music that have been programmed for you, and fit this jigsaw into the precise time allowed. The precise time for *All Ways on Sunday* was three and a half hours.

I'd had some experience in amateur theatre; I wasn't a bad actor. I decided I'd treat the program as a piece of theatre, so the thing to do was to rehearse. The night before the first program went to air, I sat in a dark studio just off William Street and rehearsed and rehearsed. I ran through the whole program three times. The curtain would go up at six-thirty the next morning.

The ABC studios were, in effect, a radio factory. Three studios sat side by side. One broadcast to the first network (metropolitan Sydney, in this case), the second broadcast to the second network (the serious specialist programs that were broadcast nationally), and I sat lonely in the third studio, broadcasting to people hundreds of miles away from the street outside. Watching over us was the studio supervisor, whose task was to make sure the whole lot worked. Who knows what he thought of me?

It's bad enough to be bad. It's much worse to know that you're bad, and I knew I was terrible. Apart from anything else, I failed my mental arithmetic. I sat helpless as ten o'clock loomed and a seamless glide into the national news was required. The piece of music I was playing had minutes to run, and I had no idea what to do.

The studio supervisor strode in, reached across my shoulder, called the time and faded down the music. Every muscle in his body was screaming: 'Who let this amateur into *my* studio?' Like the thief in the night, I picked up my belongings and scurried away.

I expected to be sacked, but I wasn't. I went through the torture again the following week, and again the week after that. Then Graham White took me to meet the network controller, who produced a mailbag full of letters, which he tipped onto his desk in a pile. The network controller told me that these were the letters of complaint—about me and the program—that had arrived to date. But the ABC would not be terminating me or the program. He was sure that things would improve in time.

I pleaded with Graham for a producer, someone who could help me straighten out this mess. At first no one was available; but then came a gift from the gods: a light entertainment producer was about to retire. It was three weeks before his big day. He could perhaps help.

He had produced the big BBC light entertainment stars. You may never have heard of Dick Bentley or Jimmy Edwards or Joy Nichols, but believe me, they were stars and he'd produced them. 'You're in uncharted waters,' he told me. 'You used to be a reporter, expert in your field. This is light entertainment, and here everybody is an expert.'

Radio works with just the one energy source: sound. He told me that most people don't 'listen' to radio, they 'hear' it; if I wanted people to listen to something, I'd have to learn how to lead them into doing that.

'Treat the whole program as a piece of music,' he told me. 'Make sure that the sound patterns are changing and keeping

Graham White (left) and Neil Inall, the driving forces behind All Ways on Sunday. *No one better understood the value of radio to regional Australia.*

people interested.' In a couple of weeks he taught me the difference between the energy generated by the human voice and a piece of music. More than that, different pieces of music generate different levels of energy. A program must be as carefully balanced as a symphony.

He sat outside my studio in the control booth for three weeks. He relaxed and read the paper and occasionally opened the intercom to coax, correct, praise or scold. He saved me and the program—and, to my shame, I can't remember his name.

These days, every regional talk/music program has a producer, someone who does the nuts-and-bolts work of cueing taped interviews or contacting live interviewees. They answer the phone and basically allow the presenter to concentrate on the job of presenting.

After those initial three weeks, I never had a producer sit with the program. The most difficult task for any presenter is to 'hear' the sound of the program they're presenting, to keep that sound in their head and to 'play' the program like a musical instrument. I would have to do it without help.

I needed to develop a technique that would allow one person working alone in the studio to continually select and cue music for presentation, while putting to air the interviews and stories, which were the heart of the program. The solution was to complete the editing of the chosen stories during the week, and decide on the time at which each would be presented. Then each story would be transferred in turn to a master tape. This simplified the business of cueing the stories to go to air. Sadly, at the end of each program the master tape was erased, ready for use again the next week. Nothing was kept.

Things were getting better, but I was unhappy. Each week I sat in a studio in Sydney and broadcast to people who were hundreds of miles away. I wasn't in touch with them. 'Please, can we do the program from a regional studio?' I begged. 'It can be anywhere, but somewhere that I know the people outside in the street might be listening.'

The idea was preposterous. Broadcast a national program from somewhere in the bush!

As it turned out, there was no technical reason why the program couldn't be broadcast from anywhere. In future years it would be broadcast from a commercial radio station in Alice Springs, before the ABC had a presence there, and even from a caravan promoted by a cigarette company, the Rothmans Special Event Van—a big caravan fitted with microphone, tape recorders, turntables and teleprinter. And the regional ABC stations all over the country that hosted me gave the program its unique flavour. Yes, we could take the program bush.

The proviso was that a PMG technician should always be on hand, in case the landline connecting whichever studio I was broadcasting from to the nearest capital city studio failed. What exactly that technician would or could do in that event was unclear, but I was always grateful of their presence.

One regular who sat with me when I broadcast from Wagga used to moonlight as a waiter at the local leagues club, and invariably brought along prawns for breakfast. In Orange, Alan Hatswell—calm, unflappable Alan—did save the day one morning when the lock on the front door to the studio collapsed, denying all access. Alan returned from a trip to the depot with a long ladder over his shoulder and we climbed in through a second-storey window.

All Ways on Sunday was broadcast from some strange places, but the trips back to the bush gave it its flavour. There were no more mailbags of complaints.

GIVE ME A HEAD OF . . .

I WAS BEGINNING TO HATE SYDNEY. I DIDN'T RECOGNISE THE PEOPLE IN the street and the sounds were all wrong. How was I supposed to connect with them? I was sick of the Kings Cross hotel, and I'd long since got over my initial gawking at the oddities crossing my path in the Cross. I was missing my wife and the kids. I wanted to go home. Then Harry M. Miller saved the day—almost. He brought *Hair* to town.

Hair was rock and roll, sex and drugs all wrapped up in a slick two-and-a-half-hour show, and Sydney couldn't get enough of it. Diana wanted to see it, needed to see it, would see it. 'Go and get tickets,' I was told.

Not only did she, like any self-respecting member of the theatrical profession, need to see this show, she also had a friend involved. Diana had directed a young, redheaded, freckle-faced James H. Bowles in an amateur production, and had encouraged him to head to Sydney and 'have a go'. James had gone and he'd landed a job in *Hair*—he was a dresser.

'A dresser for *Hair*—all those girls! It's like dying and going to heaven,' he reckoned.

Harry M. had pulled off a coup. The thought of all those naked breasts on stage sufficiently enraged Joh Bjelke-Petersen that he declared *Hair* would never be staged in Queensland. That saved Harry M. the expense of restaging the production, because half of Queensland made the trip to Sydney to see it. Each Friday and Saturday, fleets of buses would disgorge the maroon hordes onto the streets of Kings Cross, and every Sunday morning the satiated degenerates would pile in and head north again. Kings Cross loved Joh.

Diana had asked a friend to babysit our mob for a weekend. She was coming to Sydney—just get those tickets.

The young lady at the box office laughed when I asked for two tickets for Saturday night, and enquired what year I was thinking of. Tickets for *Hair* could not be had, not even for ready money.

I could have broken the bad news to Diana but I'm naturally sneaky. There were plenty of other avant-garde companies in Sydney doing cutting-edge stuff; we'd see one of them instead. She'd understand.

'Have you got the tickets for the show?'

'Yes, dear.' I wasn't lying, just being nonspecific.

I'd been living in the hotel at the Cross long enough to be on first-name terms with the bloke who drove the lift—yes, they used to have a lift driver in those days—and I introduced him to 'my wife, Diana'.

'Oh yes?' he said—nudge, nudge, wink, wink.

The weekend was not off to a good start.

I took Diana to a hotel for a meal. A wedding reception was in full swing at the bar. The bride looked magnificent as he breasted the bar, casually pushing the veil back from his face to down a schooner. Diana didn't notice . . . a little local colour gone begging.

She picked up the fact that we were heading the wrong way to get to the theatre, and I then had to break the news that we wouldn't be seeing *Hair*, 'but . . .'.

I can't remember what the show was that we saw. We had very good seats, front row; everyone else in Sydney was at *Hair*. It was very avant-garde, and a young lady wearing nothing much at all really did leave the stage and sit on my lap and feed me pieces of apple. It was very symbolic.

Diana was not amused.

We saw *Hair* restaged in Melbourne in the 1990s. What a gentle, old-fashioned little show it was by then.

GOLDEN MEMORIES

At Orange you need to be careful when you talk about early gold discoveries. The Tom families are still very much part of the community, and any suggestion that Edward Hargraves—that jumped-up usurper, that blow-in from California—found the first payable gold will get you a history lesson. William and James Tom were the men, and Hill End was the site.

There was a road connecting Bathurst and Mudgee that ran through Hill End. I'd used it once or twice; it was always a good idea to check your vehicle afterwards for the parts that had fallen off. I'd always thought it unfair that Ballarat and Bendigo had such lavish displays of the wealth brought by the gold rush, while Hill End looked forlorn.

Hill End is now in the care of NSW National Parks and is well maintained. But when Neil Inall and I went there looking for colour pieces for the pilot program of *All Ways on Sunday*, it was a very different place. Buildings were deserted and in disrepair, and it had the look of a ghost town about to happen.

We weren't having much success finding suitable 'talent' either, until we came upon a cottage that looked to be settling down on the side of the road. I guessed that originally it had been on the same level as the road, but that, every time they top-dressed, the road rose a little and the house seemed to sink a little. Inside was a lady with a story to tell.

*The Holtermann Nugget:
they sat it on grandmother's
best tablecloth and said,
'Anyone who can pick it up
can have it.'*

Look up the register for great gold nuggets, and right at the top you'll find the Holtermann. It's not strictly a nugget, the books will tell you, but at somewhere around 290 kilograms it's the largest piece of gold ever mined.

The Holtermann came out of the Star of Hope mine in Hill End. 'And it sat on that table,' the lady told us.

'This one? The one we've got the recorder on?'

'Yes, right there. My grandmother told me that the men were looking for somewhere to display it. They wanted everyone to come and have a look. Everyone was crowded into this room. They were so excited. They said that anyone who could pick it up could have it.'

We were sitting around a piece of history!

It was a fine old sturdy Victorian table. Nothing special, but, yes, it seemed strong enough to hold that great chunk of rock and metal.

'Grandmother wasn't too pleased, you know. She had her best tablecloth on the table, and they didn't give her time to take it off or anything.'

She wasn't sure what sort of tablecloth; we speculated that it might have been one of those nice crushed-velvet cloths with the little baubles around the edge. Yes, she agreed, it might have been. All these years and two generations later, her displeasure at the indignity was palpable.

'Well, they took the gold away, and the next day they came back and asked grandmother for the tablecloth.'

'So they were at least going to wash it for her,' we offered.

'No, they wanted to make sure there wasn't any gold left, caught up in the cloth.'

For the record, they extracted something like 3000 troy ounces of gold from the Holtermann—around 93 kilograms. And they found even bigger pieces in that mine, but broke them up to make it easier to get them to the surface.

THE LIGHTS OF COBB & CO.

I was working in Albury, presenting the program from the ABC studios there, when a nurse from the local hospital put her head into my office one day and asked if I'd like to talk with 'the last Cobb & Co. driver'.

Arthur Robinson was in hospital. He was very unwell, and I had some reservations about asking him for an interview, but he was cheerful and ready to talk.

I told him, 'I'll stay until you tell me to leave.' And he never did. He took me back to the nineteenth century, opening a window onto work and ways long gone.

Arthur's right arm was deformed, bent. It looked to me as though he'd broken it as a kid, and that it had been roughly set or even left to set itself.

'No,' he told me, 'that's bent from holding horses.'

His lifetime of working with horses began at an age when our children are just stepping up from primary to secondary school. At thirteen he was working in the horse yards, harnessing teams for Cobb & Co.

Cobb & Co. began life with the gold rush, and its early runs served the goldmining towns. The company built its reputation on quick and dependable service. That reputation was in the hands of young kids like Arthur.

The coach teams, Arthur told me, travelled at a hand-gallop over stages that varied, but were around 10 to 12 miles. They travelled at something like 6 or 7 miles per hour. Keeping up that speed over the whole length of the trip depended on having quick changeovers at stations along the way. As a boy, his job was to make sure that happened.

'How many horses to a team?' was an obvious question. The answer was either five or seven; but the number of horses wasn't as important as the quality.

You can buy harnesses for horses these days; when you do, you'll be buying 'off the rack'. That didn't do for Cobb & Co. Arthur told me that each horse had its own harness, and that was very important if you wanted to get the best out of that horse. Part of his job was to make sure that he put the right harness on the right horse.

The next team of horses would have to be standing ready when the coach pulled in. 'You'd drop one team off and get the fresh team in, and the driver would be away in a matter of minutes,' he told me. Arthur's next responsibility would be to cool down the spent team, remove the harnesses, feed and groom the horses, and look to any repairs that might be needed.

Imagine a Cobb & Co. coach at full stretch. The picture in your mind is of a coach kicking up dust somewhere at midday, right? I got quite a surprise when Arthur told me that the coaches could travel at night. It made sense: it was cooler, and so easier on the horses.

'But how did you see at night?'

'A big bullseye lamp up on top of the coach,' he said, which 'gave a pretty good wide light'.

I laughed and said that roos were a problem with night driving these days. He assured me that things were no different then: it wasn't unusual to have a near miss with a mob cutting across in front of the horses.

Arthur drove three runs in western Victoria and southern New South Wales. He knew the road between the gold towns of Ararat and Landsborough, and the tracks to what then would have been the isolated communities of Tocumwal and Finley. He also drove the Hay–Booligal line.

People would have been in a hurry to get to the goldfields in those days, and I guessed that the coach would on occasion have been overcrowded. 'What was the usual load?' I asked.

Arthur's answer pretty well summed up attitudes in those far-off times: 'I've had up to fourteen real people. But I've carried twenty-two Chinee.'

CHINESE GOLD

The strangest story I ever covered for *All Ways on Sunday* began with a small parcel the size of an audio cassette. Inside was not the expected tape, but what proved to be two ingots of solid gold. Attached to the package was a note saying that if I presented the contents and the note to a particular person at Prouds, the jewellers in Sydney, it would be proof that he could tell me their story. Even more intriguing was the suggestion that if I wanted to make contact with the sender, I would have to do so via telegram to a post office in North Queensland.

Whoever sent that package certainly knew how to prick a journalist's interest.

It was the early 1970s, the Whitlam government, having just come to power, had announced its plans for decentralisation. Gough was already talking about Albury–Wodonga becoming the new Brasilia, and the ABC must have decided that it would make a token gesture in that direction. I was being moved from Canberra, where I'd been working as both the rural political reporter and the presenter of *All Ways on Sunday*, to Albury. At least one national program would be broadcast from this would-be mega-city.

Of course I wanted to know the mystery of the little package, but I couldn't get from Albury to Sydney and back in time to present the following Sunday's program. I asked a colleague to unlock the secret for me. I couldn't believe the result.

The package had been sent by a Mr Zarb, who claimed that the gold was a small part of a cache of Chinese gold and artefacts he'd discovered at the old Palmer River goldfield. He wanted to present the gold and the artefacts to the newly announced Museum of Australia. Could I help?

Gold was discovered on the Palmer River in 1872–73, relatively late in the gold rush era. This was in Far North Queensland, about 170 kilometres inland from Cooktown, and it was uncharted country. Northern Australia at that time was sparsely populated; unlike most other areas where gold had been discovered, no white settlement was in place. Miners would come face to face with some very hostile Aborigines.

Chinese workers in the area would be different too. Most were brought to the fields as indentured labour controlled by 'tongs' (Chinese cultural organisations). Many of them had no idea where they were; they thought they were at workings on the east coast of the United States. In time, Cooktown would become a very big Chinese settlement, home to many more Chinese than Westerners.

Initially there was no road as such to the new diggings, just rough bush. Early on, there were cases of miners starving to death along the track, with a billy of gold beside them but no food. This is tropical country, so would-be miners faced the added difficulty that they'd be unable to move in the 'wet', while pack animals would be short of feed in the 'dry'. There's a marvellous story from the area of a packhorse being found wandering at the point of starvation, fully loaded with rich quartz. Who loaded the animal, and where the quartz came from, no one knew.

To add to the romance of the place, the track led through a pass in the range that came to be known as Hells Gate. It's a very narrow pass, just wide enough to get a pack animal through; even today, if you visit the pass—and not many people do—you'll see the rub marks of the pack-saddles on the rocks. It's the ideal place for an ambush, and the local Aborigines developed a fearsome reputation for defending their country. At Battle Camp a party of warriors took on Europeans armed with rifles; they stood and fought, with great loss of life.

The story grew that these natives were cannibals. Now, cannibalism among Aborigines has always been hotly denied, but if you read the reports of early government officials in the area, they certainly *believed* it went on. Whether they ate anyone or not, and there's no evidence that they did, they certainly hunted Europeans and Chinese alike, in defence of their country.

Any story that came out of the Palmer River goldfield had to be a good yarn. I put the bare outlines of what I knew about my mystery package to air and was amazed by the result. Almost immediately I had a phone call from the director of the as-yet-unbuilt Museum of Australia. He guessed that all this was a joke, but wanted to be sure. I promised him that, as far as I knew, this Mr Zarb was genuine. Certainly the gold was. With the director's say-so, I responded to my mysterious explorer.

Telegrams went to and fro, and I learned that my informant had already had dealings with the Queensland government. Officials had contacted him, claiming that his find amounted to 'treasure' and so was the property of the state. He might get a reward for the find, but first he had to hand it over. His response was one that he would use again and again: 'If it's yours, you must know where it is. Go and get it.'

What did he want from the museum? With an eye to history, Mr Zarb said that he wanted the collection to stay together—the gold and the artefacts. He wanted his name associated with the collection, and he expected a monetary reward, but something less than the value of the gold.

This story had great television possibilities, and I contacted John Sparks, the director of *A Big Country*, who was very interested. We started the search to find out as much as we could about this magical pot of gold. There were characters stamped into those little ingots, so our first task was to find out what they might mean. As a country, Australia had not yet officially recognised Communist China, so the ingots were taken to the Taiwanese embassy with a request for a translation. That proved to be very interesting.

The gold, we were informed, carried the mark of the Black Dog Tong. That tong still existed and was active; we were advised to put the gold back where we'd found it.

So there was no doubt that it was Chinese gold.

I had a photograph of the ingots, and many years later, when I was working for the Australian Wheat Board, I showed it to a Chinese friend at the board who'd just saved the company from making a monumental cultural blunder in China. She was very interested and asked how I'd got the photo, and I told her the story. Chinese characters can be read in a number of ways, she told me, but these clearly said: 'Black dog. Say nothing.'

It's almost certain that the Chinese were sending gold from the field back to China, and the suggestion is that they did so in a number of ways. The more inventive stories centre on brass buttons and burial urns.

The story goes that Chinese workers might be repatriated in two ways. If they completed their indenture, they'd be sent home in a new coat with a double row of brass buttons—which were really made of gold that had been lacquered to look like brass. On the other hand, if they died in this godforsaken country, then their spirit would wander the earth. They had to be returned to China. They'd be buried, disinterred after a period of time, and their bones folded into a clay burial urn for return home. The long bones that went into those urns—so the story goes—would be hollowed out and filled with gold.

There are reports of 'war' breaking out between rival tongs on the goldfields and at Cooktown. Out-of-luck European miners were recruited into private Chinese armies.

It was becoming more and more possible that Mr Zarb may have stumbled on something of considerable cultural, if not financial, significance. The museum was interested and *A Big Country* was interested; negotiations continued.

Mr Zarb proved quite willing to be part of the TV program, but he raised an important difficulty. Where the gold lay was very inhospitable country, he claimed, and we would never get a film crew in.

Not to be outdone, John Sparks approached the Army; because of the involvement of the museum, perhaps they would arrange for a helicopter to take the crew in and the gold and artefacts out. That was agreed to. The museum was happy to meet the cost of Mr Zarb's reward. Given that he was gifting all this to the Australian people, there was no question of it being classified as 'treasure'. Let final arrangements begin.

Up to this stage, the system of exchanging telegrams had proved clumsy but workable. However, now the system broke down. I had no reply to one telegram, nor the next, and then, out of the blue, a very strange message—in essence: 'Who are you? I've never heard of you in my life.'

Something was very wrong. I pressed him. It was pointless trying to say that none of this had ever happened; after all, I had seen the gold. What was going on? Was more money required?

Mr Zarb responded with a very strange tale. He lived out in the bush, and one night he had some visitors—Chinese visitors. In his words, they 'told me that I had something that belonged to them and they'd like it back please'.

He tried the trick that had worked so well with the state authorities. 'I told them,' he said, 'that I hadn't moved anything so, if it belonged to them, they must know where it was. Go and get it.'

That didn't work. His visitors told him that if he had a look inside his house, he'd see that his wife and children were missing;

when they got their gold, he'd get his wife and children back. They got their gold.

How much of all this is plausible?

If you go to the Palmer River field these days, you'll find plenty of large mining machinery rusting away. How they got that equipment there is nothing short of miraculous, and there's plenty of evidence of Chinese occupation.

There's no doubt that on this field, as with most others in Australia, a relatively small number of Europeans were able to bar the Chinese from working quartz gold. The Chinese concentrated, as was their custom, on working and reworking alluvial deposits. The tongs were certainly very active in the area. Now, tongs are not criminal organisations—they are business and cultural associations—so it's probable that they collected and branded gold the association had mined. My small ingots were proof of that at least. But the Chinese were never forced from the field. Would a well-organised tong simply walk away and forget that it had left a quantity of gold behind?

Did Mr Zarb ever find anything more than some curios and a handful of gold? I can't answer that question. I never met the man. I don't even know if that's his real name, but it would be a very strange individual who would enter into the complicated charade that our search for Chinese gold became, if he knew that he'd have nothing to present at the end.

The story died, but my conversation with Mr Zarb continued, now by letter. He wrote to me claiming that Prouds had cheated him. They'd taken the news of his discovery to Hong Kong, seeking a buyer, and that had never been his intention. This, he claimed, was how the tong came to know about his discovery.

The prospect of *A Big Country* documentary had obviously pricked his interest. This story, he thought, could make a good film—I agreed—and perhaps there was money to be made from a film?

He had a fairly inflated idea of what the person who provided the 'idea' for a script might be entitled to, and no idea at all how to go about writing a script. Perhaps I could help?

I know my limitations. I was not the writer he was looking for, and that was the end of the conversation.

I have no idea what happened to Mr Zarb, but I hold dear a little colour photograph of two Chinese gold ingots marked 'Black dog. Say nothing.'

HARBOURMASTER

SHE WAS THE HARBOURMASTER. TRUE, SHE WAS SELF-APPOINTED, AND her port no longer boasted even a jetty, and the boats that had once claimed it as their home port were at best rotting hulks dotted along the banks miles down the river. But the ghosts lingered, and she was tending to them.

The building was so out of place that it had to have a story to tell.

Moama in the 1970s was a tiny town on the New South Wales side of the Murray. Its past was behind it, but this building showed that something important had happened here. I climbed out of my car to have a look and was just starting to wonder whether a rummage through the interior would count as trespass, when the old lady cried, 'Are you looking at the warehouse, dear?'

I wondered later whether she spent her days looking through her front window, hoping someone would stop so she could claim her harbour dues—which was the chance for her to talk.

'Is that what it was?' I asked.

A silly question. The answer was obvious, but it got the conversation started.

'It's cold,' she said. 'Come inside and have some soup.'

It was cold, and the soup was ready and hot. I felt sure I wasn't the first to walk into that parlour.

'It used to be bigger and busier than the Port of Melbourne,' she said. Her pride was infectious; it was stoked just a little by the

94

impact of the interstate rivalry that had very much driven things when her port was abustle.

She launched into stories of men and boats long gone, and of the fierce competition for cargo that drove reckless behaviour. These days cars stream across the bridge at Corowa, linking the two former colonies, without so much as a glance at the little customs shed building standing sentinel on the southern side. But, yes, things were very different when there was a battle for trade between the Port of Moama and the Port of Echuca, which faced each other from opposite sides of the river.

'There were terrible accidents,' she remembered. She once saw a body hanging in a tree high above the river. 'Blown there, he was, when the boiler exploded. His belt caught on a branch and he just hung there.'

'How many boats would have called at Moama?' It was the obvious question.

'Oh, hundreds.'

'Hundreds? That's a lot of boats . . .'

'Yes, hundreds. Come next door to the warehouse and I'll show you.'

As we walked across, she told me with great pride that her port had seen the first boat, the *Mary Ann*, come up the river. Hundreds—yes, hundreds—of boats had followed her. She told of barges piled high with wool going down the river, and 'just about everything you needed coming back up the river'.

It all seemed a little topsy-turvy to me. Here we were, about halfway along the river border between New South Wales and Victoria, and she seemed to be turning her back on Melbourne and Sydney as sources of supplies.

She was patient. 'There wasn't any railway.'

Oh, of course. I should have thought of that.

'So everything had to go down to, or come up from, the Port of Goolwa, in South Australia. Until they put the railway into Echuca.'

I sensed that conversations about Echuca and railways on the other side of the river might not be welcome, and anyhow we were now at the door of the warehouse. She had a key and we went inside.

I'm not sure what I expected—stand-up desks sporting inkpots and steel-nibbed pens? But there was nothing, just a huge barren waste and pigeon shit, which pocked the dozen or so old ledgers that were scattered about on the floor.

'It's a shame.'

That's all she said, but I got the sense that she was talking about more than just an abandoned warehouse. She was talking about the life that had been on the river—her early life, which was now all gone. I bent down to pick up one of the old ledgers for a look.

'Take it,' she said. 'Take it.' She wanted someone else to hold onto the memory.

There was nothing of great importance in the ledger. What did I expect? It was just a list of goods received and prices, all very neat and obviously written with one of those steel nibs.

I handed her the ledger and suggested that it should be preserved in a museum or a library. It was part of the building. It wouldn't mean anything if you took it away.

She locked the door. I got back in my car and the old lady returned to her soup and her vigil.

BUSH PILOTS

Bush Pilots Airways doesn't fly anymore, which is a pity. The airline was so Australian, so relaxed and it flew into those places we automatically think of when we say Australia. They flew me to Cooktown twenty years before the company went out of business.

Before we took off for the return flight, I watched the hostess as she walked down the centre aisle of the old DC-3. She was numbering us off like sheep in a pen. Something distracted her, and with a shake of her head she went back and started again.

I asked whether she'd ever left anyone behind. She confessed that she'd once completed her third passenger count without getting the correct number and had begun to doubt her capacity to count. The plane was warming up for take-off when a frantic hammering at the door alerted her to the fact that, yes, she was one short.

As I said, relaxed.

I had a mate on the flight back to Cairns. He was an Aboriginal stockman dressed in his finest. Everything from his satin shirt to his boots was new. He shone, and he was looking forward to a great week in Cairns. He had the window seat and the view out over the reef, which was stunning. I don't know how high the pilot was flying, but he was certainly doing his best to give us a view.

My mate and I were chatting as the hostess paraded down the aisle clutching an armful of stubbies in stubby holders with the query: 'Do you reckon you could keep one down?'

We both thought that could be a possibility.

As I remember it, he finished his stubby just before me and pulled it from the stubby holder. He looked about for a second or two, perhaps for a replacement, and then, with a sharp tap of his elbow, he knocked the window of the old DC-3 open and dropped the empty stubby out. An empty stubby is the most useless thing in the world, right?

I was a touch concerned at the sudden access to fresh air, and so was the hostess. She came and had a look and scampered forward at a rate of knots. The pilot or co-pilot came back, roared into my crestfallen mate and moved us to other seats.

I kept thinking about that reef down there and the things swimming around it, and I worried that we might join them if that window fell off and hit something vital. I carried a 'bunny' knife with me then (try that on an airline now). Since the window was flapping, I tried to jam it with the knife. That brought me a rocket from the hostess, and a firm message: 'Get back to your seat!'

Of course, those old 'Biscuit Bombers' were close to indestructible and we landed at Cairns without any problem. The wallopers were waiting for my mate there, and they carted him away, still resplendent in those holiday clothes.

BROKEN BLADE

JACK BENNETT WAS ON A MISSION. HE WAS A LOCAL FARMER INVOLVED in local politics, but I'd never seen him before he walked into the ABC's Orange studio. In the months ahead, I'd come to know that I'd met a truly good man.

Jack wanted to do something for his mates. He wanted us to remember them. Not that there was much chance that we'd forget them, but over time memories fade, and these men deserved to be remembered. His mates were members of Australia's 8th Division, Japan's prisoners of war.

Jack's generation and his children's still remembered the pictures of walking skeletons and the stories of barbarity. But the war was over; we'd moved on. Japan was now a trading partner, a tourist destination. And Jack reckoned that was the way it should be— forgive, but not forget. That was why he wanted to do something.

All those years ago, his mates had been brought together from around the country to train in the middle of a Bathurst winter to go to war in the tropics. As an officer and a local, he remembered being sent to pick up a mob of Queenslanders who'd been ordered on a route march clad in tropical gear—Bombay Bloomers (those terrible Army-issue shorts) and short-sleeved shirts—in temperatures guaranteed to neuter the proverbial brass monkey. They'd become bushed and were in a bad way.

'The Army nearly finished them before it shipped them off,' he remembered. 'Planning wasn't a strong suit.'

If you go down to the Bathurst Showground, you'll find, at the entrance to the sheep pavilion, plaques commemorating the units that trained there during the Second World War. From 1940 all the way through, a steady stream of young Australians did their time at Bathurst before going off to war. The men of the 8th Division should have their memorial in Bathurst.

Jack had very definite ideas about what sort of memorial that should be. Not some flamboyant bronze 'never forget' type of memorial. He wanted something simple, something to honour the dignity of the soldiers who'd fought the enemy's attempt to strip them of their dignity. But first he needed to raise the money, and that was where I came in.

They'd set up a national committee to organise the memorial, and Jack was its president, but the hard part was coordinating things on a national scale. Members of the 8th who'd made it home were scattered far and wide, so Jack couldn't believe his luck when a national radio program finished up in his front yard. Here was his conduit. Jack used the program to appeal and to raise funds. *All Ways on Sunday* was a gift, and he used it to keep his mates up to date with the progress of the memorial.

Off-air, he talked to me of his experiences at the Changi prisoner-of-war camp. He told me of escape attempts, and the futility of the escapes—escape to where? The retributions and the work of Major General 'Black Jack' Galleghan to stand between the Japanese and his men. But he wouldn't put any of this to air. It wasn't his style.

He told me of the time he had been summoned before the Japanese colonel, never a good thing. Jack couldn't think what he might be in for, but it wasn't going to be pleasant. And then he was handed a letter.

It was the Emperor's birthday, the colonel explained, and by way of celebration mail would be issued to the prisoners. Jack had been chosen as the one to receive this piece of Japanese largesse, and here was his mail. A glance told him that this wasn't a letter from home;

it was an official missive of some sort. But why was the Australian government writing to a Japanese prisoner of war? A promotion?

He took his mail and saluted, and when he was back in his hut he opened his message of comfort. It was his income tax assessment.

Jack was excited when he received the design for the memorial. It was exactly what he was hoping for. It would be carved from local pink granite. It represented, he told me, a bayonet tested in battle, with its tip broken off—but it would still show the armourer's mark, a figure eight broken across the top and a sword cross. Bowed but not beaten. It said symbolically all that needed to be said about his mates.

The Broken Blade Memorial would be erected at the entrance of the Bathurst Entertainment Centre, and of course there would be a celebratory dinner to mark the event. His mates would be getting together, and he wanted me there alongside him.

Now, lots of people befriend you when you're producing a national radio program and can be of use to them, and most immediately forget you when you've served your purpose. But not Jack. I was part of the organising committee, he told me. I deserved to be there when his mates saw how they'd be remembered. Jack took a good deal of convincing that this was their day, his day, and that I deserved no part of it.

He tried again later, insisting I should be there when a special dinner was held for the survivors of the Sandakan Death Marches. Only six of more than 2000 British and Australian prisoners of war survived a deliberate march to the death towards the end of the war. They were members of the 8th. They should see how they'd be remembered. Again I had to politely tell Jack that I had no right to even a tiny share of that terrible story. He truly was a generous man.

The Broken Blade Memorial to the 8th Division was unveiled on 15 August 1970, twenty-five years after the surrender of Japan in the Second World War. Time was already getting on.

Time had passed, too, when a Japanese trade delegation was due to make a visit to Jack's shire. He inspected the room where a formal lunch to welcome the guests was laid out, and noticed that the Japanese flag was displayed wrongly. He had the error corrected. When one of his fellow councillors suggested that Jack should be the last to be concerned about the Japanese suffering a minor slight, he told him what he told me on many occasions: never forget, but forgive.

The Broken Blade Memorial is gone. In 2008 a young bloke who'd had too many swung on that broken tip as a skylark. It could be that the frosts of 38 winters had weakened the blade's connection to its plinth, but in any event it crashed to the ground and was smashed beyond repair.

I was terribly upset when I heard the news, and I thought of Jack, gone by then, I guessed. How would he feel? How would his mates feel?

They replaced the memorial, of course. But, as they said at the rededication ceremony, 'It's a replacement. The original's gone forever.'

OUR HENLEY

I'D NEVER BEEN TO ALICE SPRINGS, AND SO I WAS EXCITED WHEN I WAS invited to present *All Ways on Sunday* there in the early 1970s during the Henley-on-Todd Regatta. I wanted to see the country and I wanted to meet the larger-than-life characters who I was sure peopled the place.

But I found I wasn't ready for the Alice.

I'd been delivered to a modern hotel and my welcoming guide was taking me for a quick tour of the centre of town. He stopped in front of an imposing, obviously colonial building to remark, 'That's Flynn's hospital. We nearly pulled that down.'

John Flynn. Flynn of the Inland, with his vision of providing the 'mantle of safety'. I'd learned all this by rote at school. The flying doctor—a national hero on his pedal radio.

'We suddenly realised that it was about all of the old Alice that was left,' my guide continued. 'Just as well, eh?'

Alice was booming. The country was prosperous, and we were at the beginning of a great new industry, the tourist industry. Tourists need things to be neat and organised. They want to be comfortable and they've got a limited amount of time. It's a case of 'show me quick' and Alice was being set up to deliver.

We drove out of town for a quick look at Heavitree Gap, and here was another shock. My only reference to this country had been Albert Namatjira's paintings. With the arrival of the Western Desert dot paintings on the art scene, Albert's traditional landscapes have been pushed into the background, but they'd been standard fare on Christmas gift calendars for years. I saw them as attractive, of course, but obviously an interpretation. The country couldn't be that colour. It couldn't look like that.

It did. It does.

I asked why the place had been called Heavitree, and my host wasn't sure. We speculated that the 'heavy tree' might have had something to do with the gallows, and struggled to make a connection. It wasn't until years later that I discovered that this stunning landscape had been named for a school, Heavitree School, in Devon, England. Connect those dots if you will. Alice was refusing to match my expectations.

Over the next couple of days I rode with taxi drivers who recounted how they'd pick up 'Old Albert', who wouldn't have the money to pay the fare. 'He gave me one of his paintings, you know,' they would say. 'I just chucked it in the bin. Silly, eh?' Albert must have given a lot of paintings away, and the taxi drivers must have been lamentably ill-informed about the value of those bits of paper.

I had introductions to bush 'characters', who spun me wonderfully improbable stories over glasses of rum, and they were dutifully recorded and stored away for the program. But I couldn't help wondering whether everyone wasn't trying a bit too hard.

Henley-on-Todd was something else. Everyone in Australia must by now have seen images of this nonsense regatta in the dry bed of the river, but nothing you've ever seen on film can capture the spirit of the thing. This is a marvellous and clever piece of entertainment. It has a nice 'larrikin' feel about it that tourists expect—and, best of all, it's the tourists themselves who provide most of the entertainment.

We've all seen footage of feet protruding from the bottom of 'sailing boats' held waist-high as the crew plough up the sand of the river, but we never see the halfway mark. That's the spot where the 'boats' have to turn; all too often they suddenly discover that they're turning right into the path of a competitor. It was sheer genius to design a course where collision is inevitable.

The action never stops. There's an event for the so-you-think-you're-strong men, who are invited to 'paddle' up the course using a shovel for propulsion, and there are events for the kids. The noise never stops, and the supply of beer seems inexhaustible.

I noticed that there were supply trucks fully loaded with the amber fluid parked ready in the streets. Unlike the Todd, the pubs would not run dry.

During the week, I met an old-timer who described the days when the river did run, when the Alice was cut off from the outside world and food supplies became problematic. Trying to be funny, I asked him what he thought Alice might do if it ever ran out of beer.

He looked thoughtful for a while, sucked on a hollow tooth and assured me, 'We'd probably drink Swan.'

I wondered what John Flynn would have thought about this modern Alice.

Flynn himself was all about change. His idea to use aircraft to provide medical assistance was revolutionary. That marvellous invention the pedal wireless, developed by Flynn's offsider, Alf Traeger, was cutting-edge stuff. Even Flynn's hospital, the last bit of 'old Alice' that they'd almost pulled down, featured a marvellous 'modern' cooling system. He was certainly in favour of change, so of course he'd have understood. But the thing was it had all happened so quickly.

When I was there, Flynn's ashes had been laid to rest at the edge of the town, under one of the Devil's Marbles, a huge boulder that had been brought there from 400 kilometres away as a fitting memorial. It was a symbol of the outback, the country he'd served so well. No one at the time bothered to ask the Aboriginal custodians whether it was appropriate to disturb one of their sacred sites to pay homage to a white man.

Years later, 'his' stone was returned to its original site, and another boulder took its place. That seemed to neatly capture the Alice enigma.

MAN WITH MULE

DURING MY WEEK IN THE ALICE FOR THE HENLEY REGATTA, I'D BEEN told to visit an old bushman living at the old-timers' village. 'Take him a case of stout,' was the advice. 'He loves a drop of stout.' I got a grin from the bloke in the bottle shop when I placed the order; he knew where I was going.

The old fella lived in a little hut, and I was to discover that similar little huts were dotted around the site. Modelled on a boundary rider's hut, they'd been placed so you could stand on your doorstep and not see any others.

Inside was a small living area, and on one wall was a long, narrow, old-fashioned photo—a 'fish eye' photo. It depicted a donkey team, and the man I'd come to see was standing proudly at the head of his team. All he was wearing was a hat, a pair of boots and a long, but not quite long enough, beard. He had a mule beside him, and he told me that that mule was his bread and butter. Now, this was a bit more like the romantic bushman I'd hoped to find.

Within a couple of kilometres of where television cameras were recording the goings-on of tourists in a dry riverbed, I was meeting a man who claimed to have made the first road in the Territory. While jet planes were delivering the next batch of the curious to modern hotels, I was sitting in a boundary rider's hut learning the difference between horse teams, camel teams and donkey teams.

They didn't get on, he assured me. Donkeys didn't like horses or camels, and the feelings were mutual. I wondered whether it was the animals or their human masters that was the problem. The camels were largely in the hands of the 'Ghans'—handlers brought from every country where the beast had been worked—and they were known to undercut the prices charged by the horse owners. For his part, he reckoned that donkeys worked harder and were less trouble.

He would make his road by dragging along a sort of plough or grader, and I guess it did no more than follow established tracks. For provisions he had to go to the stations he passed through, but that came at a cost. He had to sing for his supper, and it was his mule that did the singing. Cattle working then was a brutal business. Cattle were caught and manhandled for castration and branding, and a man with a mule was a useful addition to the workforce. He used his mule to pull up young cattle and was rewarded with a supply of provisions. He was a solitary man, his best mate a mule.

His final story was about an occasion when he'd ridden that mule into a station to pick up his supplies. There he was dressed as I'd seen him in the picture, astride a mule with a chaff bag across the mule's withers, ready for the supplies. He explained that it was a hot day; he thought it might have been a Sunday morning. In his words, 'The boss came out, took a look at me and said, "Jesus Christ! It's Jesus Christ!"'

It was a great interview—a wonderful piece from a time that was just out of reach, but which could have been a hundred years ago. And it had a great punchline. But could I put the boss's words to air on a Sunday morning?

Now comedians use language that would make a sailor blush and no one turns a hair, but at that time putting the wrong word to air was a sackable offence.

I thought about it and decided it was too good not to air. Nobody complained. It could be that no one noticed.

LIGHTNING FAST

I was once invited to start a race. Nothing sanctioned by the AJC, I'm afraid, but the first billy goat derby at Lightning Ridge. It was one of those 'seemed like a good idea at the time' things. The main street was the venue, and anyone and everyone could, and did, enter.

If you know anything about the country around the Ridge, getting a starter wasn't a problem—but building the cart the billy was going to pull might be.

There were some ingenious contraptions, and some that looked as though they really might work. No expense had been spared in grooming the entrants—there were ribbons around horns; indeed, there were some pretty impressive horns—but, unfortunately, not much attention had been paid to trackwork.

Stewards eventually marshalled the field and assorted kids climbed into assorted contraptions and grasped the reins. The spectators pressed forward, forming a solid barrier down each side of the track—they'd come to regret that—and cameras flashed. I raised the starter's flag in professional fashion and the field took off.

Some went back the way they'd come. To others, those barriers of human flesh were nothing more than flimsy impediments between them and home in the red stony hills around town. Did I mention that there were some pretty impressive horns?

As I remember it, the winner made it about three-quarters of the way down the track before tipping the cart and its contents over. Close enough.

JIMMY HEREEN

I BUMPED INTO JIMMY IN ALICE SPRINGS, AND I DOUBT IT WAS AN accident. Jimmy could tell a tale and he liked an appreciative audience. Jimmy Hereen was a yarn spinner, a miner and a bushman, and you could put his attributes in any order you liked and you wouldn't be wrong. He spun me and my listeners some old yarns and introduced us to some Territorian lore that was new to me, if not to some of them.

He backed his claim as a bushman with an account of being sent out to retrieve the body of a young public servant who, it was assumed, had got bushed and perished. Jimmy had dismissed the task with a sniff and the observation that it was 'a waste of time'. To him, there were only two possibilities.

Either the young man had made the fatal error of camping in a creek bed and been caught when the creek came down. In which case, 'his body will be up a tree somewhere and we'll never find it'. Or he'd simply done a 'perish'. In which case, 'the dingos'll have found the body and it'll be in a dozen different places'.

An unforgiving place, the Territory, and Jimmy should know—he had a mine 'out there in the Tanami'.

Jimmy spun me the old yarn of the importance of rum as a bush measurement. If you've never heard it, then let me tell you: the concept is as important in any four-wheel driver's arsenal as the recovery winch.

If you drive in the Territory, it's a given that somewhere, sometime you'll get bogged. The severity of that dilemma can be a measure of your status when discussing similar incidents with other unfortunates. The universal measure of catastrophe is the number of bottles of rum needed to be consumed before you free yourself. A really bad bog might be a four-bottler. To the best of my knowledge, no one has ever claimed the disastrous situation where the supply of rum was exhausted before the vehicle was extracted.

What I didn't know was the significance placed on rum as emergency rations, nor the cunning methods used to ensure that, no matter what the disaster, those rations would arrive intact. Jimmy told me that in the days of camel loads, to make sure that emergency rum arrived in good order and condition, each bottle would be pushed into a loaf of bread for protection. He claimed that the practice has continued up to the present day's helicopter drops.

It made perfect sense, he argued. 'If the rum arrives safely, you can eat the packing. If a disaster has occurred, you can at least suck the rum through the bread.' Irrefutable bush logic.

Jimmy was in partnership with an Aboriginal mate in a mine 'somewhere out in the Tanami'. There are gold and silver deposits in the Tanami Desert, but Jimmy never specified which they were chasing. He did, however, spin a great yarn at his own expense about a disaster at that mine.

Things had been going well at the mine, and there was a need for some further development—some blasting was needed. Jimmy confessed that he'd decided 'to lair off a bit'. He'd bought an electronic blasting device: 'You know, one of those ones you see in the cowboy movies.'

His Aboriginal mate had never seen anything as high-tech as this, and Jimmy planned to spring a surprise on him. In his words, the two of them worked down in the mine, placing charges in the appropriate shot holes and wiring them up. Then they returned to the surface, where Jimmy grabbed his newfangled device, turned to his mate and said, 'Watch this for a bit of whitefella magic,' and pushed firmly on the plunger.

Nothing. Nothing at all happened.

'I went cold,' Jimmy recalled. 'I mean, there's got to be a connection off somewhere down there and someone's gotta go and find it. I don't mind telling you, it took a bit of talking to myself to get me back down there.'

He did eventually pluck up the nerve and started his descent. He carefully counted the number of rungs on the ladder down into the mine—thirteen. A thought crossed his mind: 'That's the same number the condemned man climbs up to the gallows.'

Jimmy checked everything thoroughly and could find nothing amiss. He climbed back into the sunlight with relief, to be greeted by his mate, who said: 'I think this thing's fucked, Jimmy. I've been pushin' it, pullin' it all the time you been down there. Nothin'!'

TED EGAN

Ted Egan and I met for the first time in the bar of a pub in Horsham, in western Victoria, in 1970. Ted was coaching music out of a cardboard box and I was putting together a segment for *A Big Country*. Ted was a bonus, and we worked him into the story.

We met again in Canberra, where Ted invited me to join him in writing a film script about a celebrated clash of cultures that happened in the Top End in the 1930s. On the face of it, this had been a case of mass murder: a group of Aboriginal men had fallen upon a party of Japanese trepang fishermen and speared the lot of them.

Beneath the surface, though, it was a much more complex business. The case was clouded by unanswered questions. It may have been that they were warriors simply protecting their country. There was no attempt to take the attack further afield, and a neighbouring party of white Australian fishermen was never threatened. Was it true that the Japanese had interfered with the local women?

The attack had taken place at a time when there were considerably more Aborigines than whites in the Territory; a white trooper who was sent out to investigate the situation was speared and killed. Nervous might be one way of describing the white population at the time.

I wasn't up to the business of writing a film script, and the idea of collaboration died. Much later, Ted earned a Master of Arts degree for his carefully researched account of the incident, and would have been pleased to be involved in a recent documentary uncovering some of the facts behind the story.

I admire Ted. I'm completely unmusical, so his ability to conjure music from a beer carton never fails to amaze me. I admire his ability to write politically charged songs, such as 'Gurindji Blues', and have people of all dispositions happily sing along with them. And I admire his integrity. Employed as an Aboriginal Welfare Officer in the Northern Territory, he resigned from the job when he could no longer agree with the philosophy of the department.

It seems to me that he has a happy knack of being able to respect Aboriginal culture and explain it in the most practical terms.

After an unexplained death in a camp, an Aboriginal group might burn the camp and move on somewhere else. 'You might call it witchcraft,' Ted once told me, 'but it makes pretty good sense. Who knows what infection might have killed that fella?'

He once showed me a pair of 'Kurdaitcha shoes'. The shoes are made from human hair and feathers, and are worn by a man on a mission of revenge. Myth says that the shoes leave no tracks. 'Not a bit of it,' Ted told me. 'They leave very definite tracks for anyone who knows what to look for, and the Kurdaitcha man is not invisible, he's just painted in a particular way. If you see a Kurdaitcha, you recognise him for what he is; you know you shouldn't see him, and so you don't.'

Ted Egan isn't above poking a bit of fun at himself. He told me of a fishing trip he had with an old Aboriginal mate. They'd hooked a beautiful barramundi, and Ted was looking forward to seeing it cooked in the traditional style, wrapped in a coating of mud and baked on the hot coals. Imagine his disappointment when his mate opened his tucker box, produced a roll of aluminium foil, added a dab of butter and rolled the parcel up for baking.

When Ted protested that he was looking forward to eating in the traditional way, his mate enquired: 'Do you like the taste of mud, Ted?'

If you've never heard Ted's song 'The Drover's Boy', you should. It will bring you up with a start. At its heart is a story of murder and rape, overlaid with tenderness and pragmatism. A ballad from a time when marriage or cohabitation between blacks and whites was illegal in this country, it's a hugely complex narrative in a simple song.

Ted tried to raise the money to film the story behind the song; he reckoned he needed $7.5 million to get the job done. Ordinary people from all over the country put their money up, but not enough to have the film made. The Baz Luhrmann film *Australia* cost around $130 million. There's no justice.

There's a rougher side to Ted. He has a song called 'We've Got Some Bloody Good Drinkers in the Northern Territory', and that's exactly what it's about. I played it to air and a listener rang to complain that the word 'bloody' had been used 'at least ten times'. I played it back to check, and counted 26. All of this is by way of saying that you underestimate Ted Egan at your peril.

OLD BROOME

I KNOW THAT BROOME THESE DAYS IS A HIGH-END TOURIST DESTINATION. But I saw it before the camels strolled at moonlight along Cable Beach, yet long after it had been the centre of the world's pearl fishing industry. And I interviewed a man who, more than anyone or anything else, personified that change.

The Broome I saw had a pearling lugger proudly displayed as the focal point of what still looked like a frontier town. The shops were as you'd imagine the marketplace in some small Asian town might look, with wooden shutters that could be closed against a cyclone.

You could walk up the coast a bit and visit Anastasia's Pool and reflect on the love story of the lighthouse keeper who'd cut this pool from the living rock so his invalid wife could enjoy the sea.

Yes, you could see the wreckage of our planes that had been shot down into the harbour by the Japanese in March 1942, but they were less of a curiosity and more of a gentle reminder of how close we'd come to defeat. And the Japanese history of the town was writ large in the cemetery, where there were hundreds of (at the time) unkempt graves of young Japanese divers.

But I was staying in a comfortable modern hotel, and I had an appointment to meet a man at the centre of Broome's new industry—cultured pearls.

I've never conducted a stranger interview. This 20th-century pearl diver would meet me at my hotel at precisely 6.30 p.m. He would join me for 'one beer' and he would leave no later than 7 p.m.

He was somewhere in his mid-30s. He'd been an abalone diver 'over east', but this was the real thing. He was in Broome to make money, a lot of money, and he was investing every penny he made in the finest jade he could buy.

'Why jade?' I had to ask.

He treated me to an explanation of the different types and how you had to be careful that you were getting the real thing, but above all he was collecting pieces that were 'beautiful—there's nothing like a beautiful piece of jade'.

We got down to work. He explained that he was the diver who harvested the shell into which would be placed the tiny beads, from which the cultured pearls would grow. Cultured pearls or blister pearls, they both needed the shell that he would harvest. There was a strict quota on that harvest, and it was his job to collect it as quickly as possible.

'When the sun comes up, I go down. When the sun goes down, I come up.'

That was the way he described his working day. There was a crew on the boat, he explained, each with a job to do, and each was paid according to the amount of shell he, the diver, collected. He was at the apex of the work.

'Someone puts my diving suit on, someone takes my diving suit off,' was how he explained it. At the end of each day he was exhausted.

And now it was seven o'clock, and people would depend on him again tomorrow. 'Goodnight.'

I thought back to those graves in the cemetery and the stories they told about lives lost to 'the bends' and to cyclones. I thought of the young men who'd died so far away from home, and the magical pearls they'd collected—and of the mundane pearl shell buttons that were the real backbone of the industry.

I'd been expecting the 'romance' of an exotic industry. But instead I came face to face with business.

MAREEBA RODEO

The Mareeba Rodeo was something special. The committee went to a good deal of trouble to get me to a place I confessed I'd never heard of. They flew me to Cairns, arranged accommodation for me in Mareeba and promised to give me 'a good time'.

They delivered in spades on all counts. I got a close-up and eye-opening view of what's become a very controversial sporting event, I collected without doubt the most extraordinary interview of my career, and I was overwhelmed by the generosity of my hosts.

With free rein to 'do what I liked', I wandered through the stockyards watching the men and the cattle at work as they got ready for the 'entertainment', and I was surprised.

All stock shift about in a yard when there are people around, but these yards were unusually quiet. Men and cattle seemed to know what to expect—they'd done all this before. Even when the bulls made their last move up into the chute, most just went quietly into position. The riders weren't the only professionals here.

The young men who were about to lower themselves down onto those broad backs were much less sure of themselves. No young prima donna ever fiddled more with her gloves. I heard all sorts of muttered invocations as they settled down and first felt the bull shift under them; I watched as they practised again and again to ensure that, at the critical moment, they could get that hand free from the bull rope, the rope around the bull's withers.

For eight seconds they'd have to use that hand, and nothing else, to keep themselves on that bull. Then it and the rope had to come free.

The call of 'ready' from the chute boss would be greeted by the merest nod. Then the chute would open, and bull and rider were released for brief mayhem. After that, it was: 'Next, please!'

I thought to myself that this must have been what it was like to shuffle up from the tumbrel and onto the guillotine.

All this was 'play' to the two blokes I'd met earlier in a pub. They ran scrub bulls for a living.

One had a terrible raw, partially healed wound down the left side of his face. Whatever had caused that trauma had either taken his eye or left it so badly damaged that it had to be removed. I learned that this was the result of an occupational hazard.

Scrub bulls, they explained, were a nuisance. Missed at the mustering when the latest 'drop' of calves had been branded and the bull calves castrated, they would run with the mob as young bulls. Left to themselves, they'd breed—and if enough of them were allowed to breed, the quality of the herd would decline. They had to be got rid of.

The traditional way had been to shoot them and leave the carcass to rot, but this was the 1970s. Beef was worth money, and so these men were being paid to run down and capture these bulls by hand. The pay? A staggering $20 a bull. 'That's good money, mate—but don't you tell the taxman.'

My friends explained the action like this. 'You come up on a mob with a scrub bull in it, and you cut him out. The trick is to get up alongside of him and push him, hard. He'll run for half a mile or so, and then he'll want to fight you. He'll start moving his head about, so you step off your horse and you grab him by the tail. He'll turn to have you, and as he's turning, you pull back and away and he's off-balance, so he'll go arse over tit. Then you jump on him and tie his legs together with micky straps. You wire his nose to his brisket, and there he is—all trussed up and waiting to be winched into the truck for the meatworks.'

There was so much to take in. 'What's a micky strap?' I asked.

'Oh, just a leather strap. You wear 'em around your waist.'

The obvious question, of course, was: 'What happened to your face?' How would he react to that?

As it turned out, he was quite cheerful about relating his 'bit of bad luck'. 'I grabbed hold of this bull's tail, and the brush come away in me hand. I've got a handful of hair and a cranky bull lookin' at me. He tossed me in the air—that's how I got this.' He made the briefest gesture to the terrible gash on his face. 'Me hat comes down and he killed it. Then it's my turn, 'cept me dog got 'im.'

Dogs hadn't been mentioned up to this point, and I wondered where they came from?

'Oh, you gotta have a dog, mate, a noser—they grab the bull by the nose and hang on. But me dog missed and the bull killed him. I was a bit lucky, 'cause by then me mate here turned up, took the bull off me and got me back to town.'

I was pretty much dumbfounded, but they went on to explain the 'perks' of the job. They had a 'good boss': he brought them a bottle of OP rum and a flagon of 'Invalid' port every morning, to help 'get 'em going'.

As it turned out, they were going back to work the next morning, and I had an invitation to 'come and have a look . . . You could even have a go yourself, if you like.'

Now, I can ride and I have worked stock but somehow or other I wasn't tempted.

NEVER SAY NEVER...

I HAD NO BACKUP FOR *ALL WAYS ON SUNDAY*, BUT THE THOUGHT NEVER crossed anybody's mind that I might 'go sick', break a leg or somehow be unable to front the program come Sunday morning.

In retrospect, if I hadn't made it, my listeners would simply have had to listen to three and a half hours of classical music from the second network, or the program from the nearest capital city. No one is indispensable. But I never missed a show.

Mind you, I came close. There was the time when the lock on the front door of the Orange studio failed to open. Locksmiths aren't readily available at five-thirty on a Sunday morning; access to the studio that day was via a long ladder and a second-storey window.

I nearly didn't make it from the Mareeba Rodeo in time. I was depending on the rodeo committee to get me back to Cairns in time for the show. We were all having a great time when the president offered to 'ring your boss and tell him you're sick'.

Even when I was in the studio there was no guarantee I'd get to air. Often I'd have worked all night editing and had camped on the floor of the studio for an hour's kip. I'd always sleep with my head up against the studio speaker with the sound turned up high. The techs broadcasted music 'up the line' as a test before programming started; a brass band at full volume is a great alarm clock.

But the nearest I came to missing completely was not on a trip but at home. I was living in Wagga and broadcasting from the Albury studios, and I'd leave home at about four o'clock on Sunday morning to drive to Albury and set up for the broadcast.

Of course, it's dark at that time, and one very wet winter's morning I was steaming down the road through the little town of Yerong Creek. I'd never seen the said creek, but guessed it must be around somewhere. This morning it was right across the road, and I went into it at a considerable rate of knots. I climbed out to survey the damage and found myself up over the knees in some very cold water. Fortunately, my old Holden was still grounded, and a guardian angel in the form of a truck turned up.

The driver gave me the choice; he'd pull me out Wagga side and home or Albury side and work. I prayed the car would start and chose the Albury side. The old girl kicked over and I arrived wet and shivering at the studio just in time to go to air.

I did that show in my underpants.

SOMETHING OLD, SOMETHING NEW

THERE ARE THINGS YOU WISH YOU'D NEVER SAID. MY CALLER WAS ASKING for help in promoting the Bendigo Easter Festival, and his name was Mr O'Hoy. We weren't recording the interview—we didn't have the technology. I was taking notes so I could script a piece to use in the program.

This was going to be a big festival, Mr O'Hoy assured me, and he was very keen to promote the Chinese contribution. He told me that among the attractions would be the Caledonian Band.

In a puerile attempt at humour, I put his name and the Caledonian Band together and said something like, 'Hang on a minute. An O'Hoy as the secretary and a Caledonian Band—I think this is a bit of a leg-pull. Where are the Chinese?'

'What do you know about Australian history?' came the reply.

Smugly, I assured my caller that I was pretty well up in that department. So he asked what I knew about the Lambing Flat Massacre. Mr O'Hoy was giving me a gentle scolding for my cultural insensitivity.

I knew all about that particular incident. Lambing Flat—now the town of Young—wasn't all that far from where I was broadcasting, and it was the scene of probably the most violent anti-Chinese demonstration in our goldfields' history. In 1861, European miners on the field had attacked unprotected Chinese miners, destroying their tents, driving them from the field and killing a number of them. It took troops to put down the disturbance; the ringleaders were later arrested.

It was a bloody affair. Newspaper reports from the time talk of miners collecting Chinese pigtails—the long, braided queue of hair they wore—as trophies, some with the scalp attached. The country was on the cusp of introducing the White Australia policy.

'A lot of those Australian miners had names like O'Neil, O'Malley. We bend with the wind,' said my caller.

I was suitably chastened.

Mr O'Hoy went on to tell me about the dragon that would be dancing at the festival. He was very proud of that dragon, which had been around since the gold days.

To make sure that I was up on my knowledge of the Chinese in Bendigo, Mr O'Hoy told me the story of the joss house or temple there: it had been built in 1870 and was still very much in use. 'There's a piece of an earlier joss house in the Bendigo Joss House,' he informed me. 'Every new joss house is started with something from an older one.'

I liked that idea—one long continuation of a culture.

FILM STAR

HAVE YOU EVER WONDERED WHAT IT MIGHT BE LIKE TO BE BROUGHT home dead over the back of a horse? You have? Well, I can tell you.

Radio stations are often the focus for all the odd and unusual things that happen in a town, so funny things tend to happen to you when you work at one. Back in the 1970s, when we were enjoying a spike in Australian-made television drama, the producers found Orange.

The town and the district had plenty going for them. There was a daily air service; it was within easy driving distance of Sydney; the country looked attractive; there were some fine old houses in town and in the surrounding country; and there were droves of locals who'd be happy to play as extras. It was a producer's paradise, and one production company that found the place was making the *Boney* TV series, adaptations of the novels by Arthur Upfield centred on the doings of Aboriginal detective Napoleon Bonaparte.

Of course the casting director had to be one of my interview guests, and she told our audience that the company would be making at least two, possibly three, episodes of the forthcoming series in and around town. She'd need extras, and if volunteers would like to present themselves at such and such a hall between the hours of . . . You could already hear the scurry of interested footsteps on their way downtown.

My wife, Diana, is an actress, and she had a role in one of the episodes. As the casting director was leaving the studio, she casually asked me, 'Would you fancy being a villain for a day or so?'

Apparently a tiny part in one episode was as yet uncast. There would be two days' shooting involved, and I looked to be about the right size and shape. It's well known that the devil has all the best lines, so I jumped at the chance. I was going to see how they made movies.

The plot of this episode was simple. Two families who'd been feuding for generations in Scotland emigrated to Australia and continued the feud down under. Two brothers, the baddies—that was me and a young actor from Sydney—have been stealing cattle from the goodies, and are caught in the act. By way of retribution, the goodies decide to firebomb the baddies, who are attempting to escape in their old mustering ute. It was exciting stuff.

The director, a very nice young man, briefed us baddies accordingly: 'You're escaping in your ute when the goodies find you. They're flying a light aircraft, and they'll drop petrol bombs on you. The ute catches fire and crashes, and you'—here he pointed ominously to me—'get burned to death.'

I could do that.

'Now, there are no lines for this scene,' he continued, 'but the camera will be on you for quite a while during the chase, so could you work up some dialogue between yourselves?'

Shakespeare, move over.

I was interested in how things worked technically. I mean, surely an actual firebomb wasn't going to fall from heaven onto the ute?

'No, no,' the director explained. 'There's a petrol-soaked mattress in the back of the ute with a detonator hidden in it, and when you hit the mark, you'—and he again singled me out—'will push a button, the detonator will explode, the mattress will go up and we'll have a ute on fire.'

'What happens then?' seemed the obvious question.

'You'—my brother in crime was singled out this time—'get out of the ute, and you'—that was me again—'are trapped in the ute and burned to death.'

I'm nothing if not practical. I looked at the ute in question. It was a battered old Holden, with both the driver's and the passenger's doors removed. It looked just the thing for scrub bashing, but I noticed a flaw. The director was keen to hear about it.

'There's no door, you see,' I said. 'I don't care what happens, but if that ute's on fire, I'll get out of it. I mean, how can I be trapped?'

Sometimes it's wise to keep your mouth shut.

The ute was carted to the top of a hill. The cameraman was strapped to the driver's side so he could shoot the interior of the cab. We were almost ready to go.

'Have you fellows worked out any lines?' the director asked.

We prattled off the gems we'd rehearsed, and he was satisfied.

'Now, remember,' he pleaded, 'we can only do this once, so please don't stuff it up.'

Big Mouth again wanted to know whether the problem of the missing door had been addressed, and he told me not to worry—that had been fixed.

Action! And down the hill we rolled . . .

I leaned from the doorway, blazing away with a shotgun at an imaginary overhead plane; meanwhile, my brother and I babbled the lines we'd rehearsed.

We hit the mark. I pressed the button. There was a dull explosion, the ute leapt into the air, and a fireball belched through my door opening and into the cabin.

The crew had acted on my suggestion. They'd packed an area outside the door with fibre soaked in petrol—and it worked. There was no way I could get out that door. A slight change in lines followed.

'Fuck!' I screamed. I planted my foot in my brother's ribs and pushed him past the cameraman and out his door. I followed hot on his tail. The cameraman was left to ride the burning wreck down the hill.

The director was excited. He said it looked tremendous, very real. Pity they wouldn't be able to use all the interior shots. 'You know—the . . . expletive.'

I was chastened.

There was more excitement to come. I, or rather my body, had yet to be discovered, smouldering beside the crashed ute. That would be after lunch.

Even though I was now dead, it seemed I still needed make-up— lots of make-up. My face would have been terribly burned, and they'd want a close-up of that. The young lady responsible was enthusiastic. She applied latex rubber all over my face and made that up; she then peeled great chunks of it away. I couldn't see myself, but no one would eat lunch with me.

After lunch, my body was found smouldering beside the wreck of the ute. 'Actually still burning?' I had an interest in the answer to that question.

'Well, there'll be some flames,' conceded the director.

Mr Curiosity again wanted to know how that might be done.

'Well, you lie down and we sprinkle petrol on you and set fire to it.'

I expected him to laugh when he said this, but no—it seemed he was serious.

I was dressed in long johns and a woollen singlet that were soaked in alum as a fire retardant. My costume went on over all that, and then petrol was splashed about and I was invited to 'lie down and keep very still'.

There was no need to ask twice. I wasn't going to do this again.

I've seen the film. The flames look realistic. They were—my lack of eyelashes and fringe proved it.

Now for that scene where the hero looks manful and the pretty girl cries. That scene where the body is brought in, strapped to a horse. I was much more relaxed about this. I'd been around horses. I could ride. This would be easy.

Don't ever try it. Your backbone is bowed, and every time the horse moves, your back flexes where it's not meant to. It hurt like hell. I never scoffed at a Western again—those bodies earn their money.

THE COFFIN

It was a pub in Queensland, and in a shed at the back there stood a coffin. Not the sort of thing to set a cheerful note, I thought. I wondered why it was there.

A hangover from a time when transport was less reliable, the publican told me, and added that he wished he'd 'had one on hand once before'. There followed a story that, if it isn't true, should be.

The town had in previous years depended on the railway for all its supplies. The beer arrived that way and the service was regular—if you could call once a week regular. Plenty of other places like it.

One regular customer was 'a gentleman', the publican assured me, 'a real nice old bloke'. The old fella turned up at the pub once a month. He was a prospector. He kept himself, and whatever he might have found, very much to himself. But once a month he'd turn up at the pub for a bath, a shave, a good meal and a clean bed.

On his last visit he didn't come down to breakfast as expected, and a search found him dead in bed. Nobody knew anything about him, whether he had a family or not, and there was nothing in his possessions to give them a clue. The pub would have to bury him.

The publican rang to have a coffin added to the beer quota on the next train. That was four days away, and in the meantime they'd have to find a place for their guest. The pub cool room was the obvious choice.

The coffin duly arrived, and they set about putting their old mate to bed for the last time.

'He was a long stringbean of a bloke,' the publican remembered, 'and he wouldn't fit. I thought all coffins were the same size, but he was longer than the coffin, and when we tried to bend his knees a bit . . . well, he's been in the cool room for four days, hasn't he?'

They had a problem. The next train and the next possible coffin were a week away, and their regular had already overstayed his welcome. While they scratched their heads, the pub handyman announced that he had a solution. 'He comes back with a saw,' said the publican.

Suddenly I'm not liking where this story is headed.

'No,' the publican reassures me, 'he bores a hole in the coffin so he can cut a little square out of one end. We slip the old bloke in, and the very top of his head just pokes through the hole. He just fits.

'We put the lid on, and got his old hat and attached that to the end of the coffin. And we buried him all dignified and proper.'

STEP BACK IN TIME

NONE OF THE INTERVIEWS I COLLECTED FOR *ALL WAYS ON SUNDAY* SURVIVE. That's disappointing. Not because my work has been lost, but because the voices of the people who told the stories have been lost, and often so much of the story was not in the words but in the voice that spoke them.

In most cases, the people I spoke with let me look back one generation. I was talking with my father's generation, if you like. On a couple of rare occasions I was able to look further back, and hear the voice of a very different Australia.

Once I talked with a very old man who claimed that, as a youngster, he'd witnessed the Kelly Gang's hold-up at Jerilderie. He had a laugh as he remembered the 'strange police sergeant' cutting down the telegraph post in front of the police station. It is just possible that he did see Ned—the gang struck in 1879—though he'd have been a very young child. Most likely his memory of the event was a memory of what adults had told him.

Things were very different when I met a Light Horseman who had fought in Palestine in the First World War. Like the driver for the original Cobb & Co. coach service, he was old and ill, but his memory was sharp and, make no mistake, he'd been there.

The Light Horseman hailed from Western Australia and, as I expected, he talked about the dirt and the flies and the bond that grew between horse and rider. He complained about 'Barcoo Rot'—sores that wouldn't heal, and which he put down to a lousy diet—and the heat, and he reckoned that 'they took better care of the horses than they did of us'. He told me one story that sent a chill through me.

They were moving in a column through a town, and a beggar sat at the roadside, he said. The horseman's picture of the man was of something that was barely recognisable as human—he was clothed in rags and probably blind. The horseman was looking at this apparition when a young officer rode up. He looked down at the beggar, and then pulled out his pistol and—in the horseman's words—'gave him a pill, put him out of his misery like'.

I think it's very wrong to judge past generations by the standards of today, so I make no comment. What I can't recapture, and what you'll never hear, is the matter-of-fact way in which the old man told his story. He didn't seem to find it exceptional. It was just part of his experience of a war that's rapidly passing into Australian mythology.

COOKTOWN CEMETERY

I CAN ONLY GUESS AT WHAT COOKTOWN LOOKS LIKE NOW THAT OUR tourist industry has sandpapered the edges to fit its specifications, but when I saw it, the place was magic. Where else could you pick a ripe mango growing on what we'd call a nature strip?

I really wanted to see the town because it had been the gateway to the Palmer River goldfields, and came close to being Australia's Hong Kong—at the height of the rush it was home to many more Chinese than Europeans. It had a marvellous museum stuffed with artefacts from the goldfields, including what purported to be a miner's last words, scratched inside a tobacco tin as he waited for a gruesome end.

That part of Australia was the coastal tip of our rip-roaring west. Inland, Maytown, which grew to service the goldfields, claimed to have staged the first striptease show in the world. Salome might dispute that, and Joh would certainly never have allowed it as a boast in any tourist publication, but by all accounts the town was a hotspot before it was swept away in a flood. Divine retribution?

That history is neatly summed up in a study of the Cooktown cemetery. The plot names reveal a model of colonial convention. You'll find good Anglo-Saxon Protestant names up near the front. The Chinese are over the back. And the prostitutes are scattered freely among them all.

RUM DOES FOR LASSETER

It was Jimmy Hereen who reckoned that rum had played an important role in Australia's greatest outback drama, the search for Lasseter's gold.

Lewis Lasseter surfaced at the height of the Great Depression in 1930 with the story that he'd discovered a veritable mountain of gold . . . out there.

Exactly *when* he'd discovered it depended on the listener. It was either as recently as 1921, just nine years previous, or in 1897, 33 years earlier. The problem was that although he was an experienced sea captain, he'd used an inaccurate watch to calculate the position of this lode. Yet while he couldn't pinpoint its position, he was sure he could lead a party to it. All he needed was money, and a lot of it, to equip an expedition.

There were so many holes in Lasseter's story that it's a wonder he got a hearing, but eventually he convinced some backers to put up the money for an expedition. It set out from Alice Springs in late 1930 and rapidly fell apart. Eventually, it was reduced to Lasseter and two companions, and then Lasseter went on alone with a couple of camels. When they got away from him, Lasseter settled down to do a perish.

Enter Bob Buck, and Jimmy's story.

The news had reached Alice Springs that Lasseter was missing. Perhaps he'd found the reef? Send for Bob Buck!

Bob Buck was a bushman par excellence. If anyone could find Lasseter, it was Bob. But at the time he was at Hermannsburg, about 80 miles (129 kilometres) away. A team of camels, loaded with emergency rations, was despatched forthwith.

'Somebody made a terrible blunder,' according to Jimmy. 'When Bob checked the rations they'd sent, there was no rum. Naturally, he came straight back to Alice to remedy the situation, and that delay was the reason that when Bob found Lasseter, he was dead. Lack of rum is the reason we don't know the position of Lasseter's Reef.'

Bob had died almost ten years before Jimmy spun that yarn, so there was no way it could be verified, but even when he was alive there were people who doubted that Bob had found and buried Lasseter's body. He used to settle the argument by producing a set of false teeth from his pocket and tossing them on the table with the assertion: 'They're Lasseter's.'

And the reef?

It's pretty obvious from the accounts of the bushmen who accompanied Lasseter on his search that he'd never been in that part of the country before. But never let the facts get in the way of a good story.

Bob Buck. He'd be the man to find Lasseter, but be sure to pack the rum.

A LAND FIT FOR HEROES

JULIUS CAESAR KNEW THE BENEFITS OF LAND GRANTS FOR VETERANS. Gratitude meant they'd support you politically, and with them away in the country they'd cause no trouble. No ruler wants a trained army loose in a city after a war.

When I was a young paperboy, ex-diggers were my regular customers for *Smith's Weekly*, the diggers' newspaper. They were starting to understand the political pressure they could bring to bear, and their paper kept the pressure on politicians to honour the promises they made to returned servicemen and women. Politicians of all stripes were quick to back soldier settlement schemes after the First World War for all sorts of reasons.

'It will open new country and break up the big runs' was a frequent cry. Some believed that settling a shattered man in the peace of the countryside would help return him to health. Bizarrely, there were instances of diggers still suffering the ill-effects of gas attacks or other debilitating injuries drawing blocks of virgin country that would require years of backbreaking work before they'd be productive.

Many of our most productive farming areas were built on the back of the soldier settlement schemes, and many successful second- and third-generation farming businesses owe their start to a 'block'. But that block will have been added to over and over by the blocks drawn by the blokes who didn't make a go of it. For many, the schemes were a disaster.

I broke with the general format of *All Ways on Sunday* to produce three half-hour special programs in which I interviewed First and Second World War blockies and their wives. The programs were called 'A Land Fit for Heroes'. Of all the interviews I collected for the program, they were the only ones I was able to save. They were sent to the National Archives and have sunk without trace. They must be there somewhere; hopefully, someone in the future will come across three seven-inch tins of recording tape and wonder what is on them. They will find the voices of a generation now gone. In the meantime, I have to make do with an imperfect memory.

I floated the idea of a couple of programs devoted to the blockies, and a simple brown envelope arrived in the mail. Inside was a leather notebook that contained page after page of the most perfect history of a blockie family. Drawings were a feature. A talented artist had drawn the plants, the flowers and the animals that existed when the digger took up his block in the Victorian Mallee, and there was also a detailed history of the brutal work needed to force that country to grow wheat.

The plans of the original homestead were there, right down to the bush timber that had been used in the construction and the recipe for the wattle and daub that had plastered the walls. Family stories of good horses and good dogs were told, and the narrative widened to include neighbours, some good, some doubtful and some obviously troubled.

Which of the neighbours was caught 'fishing' in the chookyard with a long line and a small hook baited with bread? Which of the neighbours was it who, coming home from a bender and finding himself locked out, piled the morning's wood against his own front door and burned his way in?

There was a time when you'd hear some strapping young man being described as being 'fit as a Mallee bull'. Now I know why. You were rich indeed on those Mallee blocks if you owned a bull, and he got very fit walking from farm to farm, to where his services were in demand.

That book was without doubt the most beautiful and the most precious thing anyone ever sent to *All Ways on Sunday*. Written in longhand, it was designed to be passed down through the family, and yet it had arrived in an ordinary envelope, sent by ordinary mail. I sent it back registered, with a plea never to let it part from the family again.

Drawing a block might have seemed like winning the lottery, but the block was no gift. To keep it, you had to begin capital repayments within two years. It had to be fenced within three years, and you had no equity, none at all, until you'd lived and worked on your block for five years.

The great problem was that often the block you drew was too small, or it was in the wrong place. All too often it might be identified as suitable for orchards, and yet the area would be found to be frost-prone. It was a brave man who took up a block in a place called Willigobung. Or you might draw a grazing block thought to support 150 breeding sheep in a good year, but the rain never came at the right time or in the right place.

Blocks of one square mile (how impressive that sounds, but it's just 640 acres) outside the recognised boundary for arable land were offered for wheat farming, but they were never big enough to let the farmer make a living.

The mateship that had developed during the war stood the blockies in good stead. Tiny—why are all big blokes called 'Tiny'?— was a pioneer in the Murrumbidgee Irrigation Area, and he gave me a picture of how he and his mates built their farms. 'Four or five of us,' he said, 'would get together in a "mess".' They'd live together under canvas on one of the blocks, and share the business of cooking and maintaining the camp while they worked cooperatively to set up each of the farms in turn. No one would leave the cooperative until all the farms were up and running.

Tiny was not the only blockie to tell me that, on occasion, the mates would take turns at being 'the horse', harnessing themselves to the small, tined equipment when the real horse was busy elsewhere.

Cooperation was the key to the success of the blockies in Western Australia. There, a group made up of men with varying skills would be given hand tools and some sheets of iron, and sent to clear the forest by hand and start farming. Those sheets of iron were very important. They would form the group's first communal shelter; using nails to fasten them was strictly forbidden, because the iron was reserved for the roofs of the houses that each of them would build in time, and those houses would all be the same four unlined rooms.

I spoke with a lady whose husband had drawn a block in Queensland and then been forced off it. He'd recently died, and nostalgia had led her back to have one last look at the old place. 'The whole district had disappeared,' she recalled. 'There was nothing but pine trees.' Her husband wasn't the only failure.

Often those blocks threw together strange bedfellows. She remembered those four unlined rooms very well, and their former next-door neighbour, who'd become a firm friend. Her neighbour was a member of the English aristocracy who'd made the 'mistake' of falling in love with an Australian digger, and then found herself in a land and in circumstances totally foreign to her. 'She couldn't cook and so I taught her,' the blockie's widow recalled, 'and she taught me how to sew. We were two women together and we needed each other.'

You didn't have to come from another land to find the life of a blockie a foreign experience. A Melbourne lady told me how she'd carefully packed her trousseau in tissue paper before setting out to join her new husband on his block. She insisted on changing into her prettiest before she joined him in his swag on the side of the road. I can see her now as she wrung her hands: 'There was red dust through everything. I could have cried.'

And there were women with their own war memories to deal with. A lady who'd nursed diggers in New Guinea was reluctant at first to talk with me. She believed that she had a duty to keep her memories to herself. I suggested that, all these years later, she probably wouldn't be revealing anything about that campaign that was still secret, but I was wrong.

'I can remember being briefed on how to behave in captivity,' she said. 'We really thought we'd be captured by the Japanese—they were so close, and our boys weren't very good, you know.' She was talking about the militia units that were the first to go into battle against the Japanese, and her assessment was practical rather than critical. 'We got to see them, you know. We were nursing them, and most of them were only boys. Some of them didn't even know how to load a rifle.'

I was learning a lot.

'The RSL was the first effective farmers' union,' an old blockie from Griffith told me, and he had the proof. He was enormously proud of an old photo that showed hundreds of men—no longer in uniform but all still in possession of the discipline a life in the Army had drummed into them—lined up outside a government office. They were in dispute with the government office, and their leaders were inside having 'a bit of a chat', to see if they could straighten things out. They got what they wanted. Perhaps it was wise to move those troops to the country and out of the way.

The blockies were quick to play up the larrikin behaviour of their days off. I was told the apocryphal yarn of the canny bloke in dispute with the bank. He owed money on an early model tractor, and the bank was about to foreclose. Without that tractor, he might as well have given it away. In due course the bank's servants turned up in their shiny shoes to claim their prize, and he marched them grimly down to the dam, where all that was visible of 'their' tractor were the mudguards and the steering wheel sticking out of the water. 'You want it, you go get it' was the challenge. Of course, the bank johnnies declined to get their feet wet, and when they were safely out of the way, the farmer waded into the water, retrieved the steering wheel and mudguards, and put them back on 'his' tractor.

Ah, but was it really like that? More probable was Tiny's yarn about the measures he was forced to take to 'hang on another year'. He was a bachelor and enormously popular in the district. He was under no illusions as to the source of that popularity: he owned a piano. As a consequence, his house was the centre of social activity.

'When the fire broke out,' Tiny recalled, 'people came from everywhere to help, and everyone wanted to get the piano out. At one stage there's a couple of blokes pulling and I'm pushing for all I'm worth, and we're getting nowhere. We were all getting a bit singed before they gave it away and left the old goanna to its fate. Funny thing—those blokes never did work out that while they were pulling, I was hanging on for dear life. The insurance on that goanna got the next crop in.'

The brutal side of the soldier settlement schemes was summed up by an old employee of the now defunct NSW Rural Bank. It was his job, he explained, to drive from failed farm to failed farm and get the farmer to see sense and to sign the land back over to the bank.

'The signs were always the same,' he said. 'You'd see horses standing there that were too poor to work anymore, and if the horses were gone, there was no hope.' He described children clothed in garments made from flour bags, and confided in hushed tones that 'it was not unusual to see rickets'.

Remember who he was dealing with. These were the men who fought and survived on the Western Front. These were tough men with a fearsome reputation. They didn't give up. First, there was the shame of failure, and that would be compounded by the knowledge that if you gave up and walked away, you walked away with nothing. There was no compensation: you had the clothes you stood up in, and nothing else.

But the bank employee had a technique he'd use when 'Dad was being difficult'. He always took a paper bag of oranges with him on these missions, he told me. 'If Dad was proving stubborn, I'd offer the kids an orange. That always did it. They'd sign.'

THE GLOUCESTER TREE

I'D ALWAYS WANTED TO SEE THESE KARRI TREES PEOPLE TALK ABOUT. THESE giants—could they be as special as all that? After all, a tree is a tree.

I found them in the Valley of the Giants in Western Australia, and the granddaddy of them was the Gloucester Tree. I knew about this giant, reputedly the tallest living fire tower in the world, and named for the Duke of Gloucester, who was supposed to have stood and watched while blokes on their springboards cut the top out of it so they could make an observation platform. Why the fellow on the ground got the honour and not the one up the tree is beyond me.

When I got to the base of this magnificent tree, I found that you could climb it (at your own risk) for a view unlike anything else in the world—a view across the karri forest.

I slung my tape recorder around my neck and started up. 'Up' meant climbing the sort of steel pegs you used to see driven into telegraph posts. I notice from tourist brochures that now those pegs seem to be a couple of feet long, and that there's some sort of a safety wire netting in place on the climb. Not then. So far as I knew, I was alone in the world.

Alone, that is, until I got about halfway up and met a bloke coming down. I remember he was dressed in shorts and a T-shirt, and he'd chosen thongs as his climbing boots. He'd now decided that caution was the better part of valour and wanted to head back down. We debated for a while whether he'd step out and around me or vice versa.

The climb up was just a climb like that until it took me through the forest canopy. Then I was up above the trees. Yes, the view was spectacular, but every upward step from there on felt like a trespass into the territory of eagles. I was scared.

The sight of the wooden fire platform above was sweet relief—all I had to do now was push the flap up and climb onto the safety of that lovely floor. I stood there to catch my breath, wondering at the bravery of the men who'd stood on springboards up here to make this platform.

The tape recorder was useless. I picked up the mic but couldn't think of anything to say that would give listeners any idea of what I felt.

And then it hit me: I still had to go down.

The first step, they say, is the worst, and I'd have to lower myself through that hole in the floor, support myself on my elbows and find that first rung with a searching foot.

Next morning I had 'jelly legs' and walking was a real problem.

I've climbed the Gloucester Tree. I see now you can pay a fee and collect a certificate to prove it. I don't need anything to remind me I've been up there—or that I failed to bring my listeners even the faintest idea of what that experience was like.

The Gloucester Tree in the 1960s,
up there with the eagles.

THE BREWER'S TALE

WHERE WAS MARK TWAIN WHEN WE NEEDED HIM?

Here we were, a new country, with no roads worth speaking of and certainly no trains. But there were two great rivers—well, one and a half. And we had riverboats. Why no Mark Twain? Charles Dickens' sons had migrated here, for goodness sake! Couldn't they have done something?

Our riverboat era didn't last long—about fifty years—but it must have thrown up characters and stories we didn't get to hear about, probably because the places that were the centre of river traffic fell quickly into neglect or turned their backs on their previous blue-collar history.

Wilcannia was like that. In the 1970s it was not a happy town. Abandoned by its grazier community, who preferred to do their shopping in Broken Hill, its streets were full of boarded-up shop-fronts. The few substantial buildings that spoke of better times were in need of repair.

The golf club, however, offered cold beer and food, even if there was something odd about the layout of the place. When I raised this with the barman, he told me that the wall I was looking at used to be part of the brewery.

I was surprised. A brewery in Wilcannia?

'Mate, this is where Resch's started.'

And there was an old bloke in the club who could and would tell me all about it.

Oh yes, my informant stated, he knew the story well. He was part of the story. Old man Resch pushed a barrow into Wilcannia with all his gear and his boots in it. He didn't have enough money to buy a new pair.

'And he started a brewery? Why in Wilcannia?'

'The river, mate.'

Wilcannia, he told me, was the gateway to Queensland, and there were a lot of thirsty people in Queensland. There were a lot of thirsty people in Wilcannia too. It was a big place, a big port.

At that stage of my life, I'd been visiting the Darling for five or six years, and I failed to see how anyone could get much more than a rowboat up the river. But the old bloke assured me that they once traded as far upriver as Bourke, sometimes even to 'Bre' (Brewarrina).

He admitted that occasionally they'd get stuck upriver and would have to wait for a decent rain in Queensland to get them moving again, but they shipped the wool from all the big stations up the river too. Some of those old captains, he assured me, could take a boat cross-country on a heavy dew. Hmm.

But about this brewery: it was lucky I was talking to him, he told me, because he had all the inside information. He was a friend of the family—well, more like a member of the family after one particularly heroic act.

The Resches had two sons. They were having a swim in the river one day, and one of them got into trouble. The old bloke had fished him out, and old man Resch, as a thank-you, put him on the payroll for life. He not only worked for the firm, he ultimately became the head brewer.

I was beginning to learn a lot about Wilcannia. We were talking about a big town, a big river port. There must have been ten pubs in town at that time, and another brewery.

Two breweries?

Oh, yes. Resch's was called the Red Lion, and the rival was the Black Horse. Of course, the Black Horse had suffered an accident.

My newfound friend had been taking the two Resch boys out for a picnic. They were a fair way out of town when one of the youngsters noticed smoke rising from a fire back in town. 'Looks like the Black Horse is on fire. Tch. Tch.'

This story was getting better and better, but I was beginning to have considerable qualms about ever being able to broadcast any of it. Shame, Australian history untold.

It's not too difficult to check on the name Resch, and my mate had some of the story straight. Yes, Edmund did start the Red Lion in Wilcannia, and he and his brother had another two or three breweries. But since they'd already been successful miners and businessmen, and had the capital to start the brewery, they probably hadn't pushed a barrow into town, even with their boots on.

And the Black Horse? There was a Black Horse Brewery in old Wilcannia, but it hadn't operated for years—and it had been owned by the Resch brothers. Pity.

The bit about Wilcannia being a big river port was accurate, though, and they did trade as far up as Brewarrina. But I'm still not sure about getting a boat across country on a big dew.

I could have been sitting across the table from Australia's answer to Mark Twain. He just needed a publisher.

THE HILL

BROKEN HILL CROUCHED BEHIND ITS MULLOCK HEAP LIKE SOME MEDIEVAL town walled against the inroads of invaders. Here, it said, we do things differently.

They certainly did. Women gave up their jobs when they walked down the aisle—'to make sure we keep young girls in town'. Everybody got the local paper, everybody. The town was governed from Sydney but regarded Adelaide as its capital, and the union kept an avuncular eye on the workers' paradise.

I was in town to present *All Ways on Sunday*, and to cover the celebration of the St Patrick's Day races—which weren't on St Pat's Day, and the 'day' lasted three days. Different. The race meeting was only three years old, but it had already developed a reputation. 'You've never seen anything like the St Pat's Day races,' they said. I couldn't wait.

ABC Broken Hill was a little different too. John Pickup was in charge. Instead of local presenters' photos in the foyer, pride of place was given to works by five local artists with very different ways of imagining the world they lived in. They weren't yet known as 'the Brushmen of the Bush', but at least one had already developed a reputation.

Pro Hart had already been known to cut one of his iconic insects from a painting to sell as a stand-alone work. Jack Absalom was yet to become a celebrity TV presenter, and John, my host for the next couple of days, proved to be a modest, gentle man who couldn't do enough to show off what his town had to offer. For me, one of his recently completed works was a standout.

The End of the Tar said the title. It was a departure from John's signature theme of Quixote wandering the western landscape. It depicted a family car alone in a huge landscape at the exact moment the ribbon of tar reaching out from the Hill ran out, and the hard yards of the dirt beyond the city began. It was a happy painting. It spoke volumes about the Hill, and I really wanted it. I looked at the price and immediately began calculating whether I could manage it with a series of payments.

The idea of the race meeting as a fundraiser for the work of the Catholic Church in the area had emerged a couple of years earlier—but how to make it different? How to attract the out-of-town money?

The celebrations were centred on the racecourse, but there was only one day of racing. The night before the big event was a warm-up, an orgy of anything goes—this was uncontrolled gambling if you listened to the enthusiasts, or the usual crown-and-anchor charity night done Hill-style if you preferred the more sober version. Races the next day, and the final day was one of entertainment at the racecourse, 'where everything is free'. A sort of give-something-back day.

All that was a couple of days in the future, and I needed to get on with the job of finding material for a program about the Hill.

The Hill, Broken Hill, the whole reason for the place, with its great holes in the ground, the mothers of that great mullock heap—naturally that was the place to start.

I couldn't go underground, but a shop in town had been converted to give you a feel of what it might be like down there. Yes, well . . .

'That's the old mosque,' said my host as we drove past what, as far as I could tell, was a corrugated-iron shed badly in need of repair. Mosque? Oh, of course, the 'Afghan' camel drivers who had once carted the wool in this part of the country. Strange—I knew how important they were to the development of inland Australia, but I'd never thought of them as being religious. But why wouldn't they have a place of worship?

'And you know about the Battle of Broken Hill?'

I was about to get chapter and verse on the tragedy that, depending on how you looked at it, either saw the Hill suffer the first Australian casualties of the First World War or experience Australia's first terrorist attack.

New Year's Day in 1915 was celebrated in the Hill with a picnic, and it was all aboard the train for Silverton. Just out of town the partygoers came under fire from, of all things, an ice-cream cart. Fluttering above it was the crescent flag of the Ottoman Empire, and beside it stood a local butcher and an ice-cream seller. Their sultan had declared war. It was their duty as loyal subjects to wage that war.

'So it was a sort of symbolic gesture?'

'No, no. They killed four people and, of course, were killed themselves.'

The police were called in and the local rifle club volunteered its services. The battle didn't take long. The protesters/sultan's soldiers/terrorists had no chance, and must have known they had no chance. They were shot and wounded several times, but they fired to the end.

The butcher had a score to settle with a local official, but the ice-cream seller had been a mild man thousands of miles from his homeland, driven by what he saw as his duty.

The attack brought the expected reprisals. The German Club in town was burned, and when the firefighters turned up to fight the flames, their hoses were cut by a mob. Foreigners in town were rounded up and sent away to the newly established internment camps in the east. Amazingly, the mosque was untouched. Perhaps corrugated iron doesn't offer much of a threat.

Ticket prices on the picnic train were refunded.

★

Isolation, it seemed, didn't guarantee safety. The Hill had a more serious scare during the Second World War.

'The story goes they picked up a bloke out at the dam. They reckoned he was planning to blow it up or poison the water,' my host said.

For an industrial city stranded in the middle of a great arid plain, that was a sobering thought. Still, there were all those pubs.

'Why Broken Hill?' I asked.

'We were using a fair bit of lead back then.'

The visit to the dam meant I got to see the Mundi Mundi Plains. It's a tourist feature now, but then it was just a plain on the outskirts of town. Sitting in my guide's car and being told that what I could see in the distance were South Australia's Flinders Ranges, I suddenly thought that I was looking at more of Australia than I had ever seen in my life.

'And the regen—you've got to see the regen,' my host urged.

Forgive me. The fenced-off area of regenerating scrub wasn't impressive. A scraggly fence line with the rabbit-proof wire netting pushed almost to the ground in a couple of places.

'You're not supposed to go wandering about in it, but bottle collectors mine it all the time.'

The 'regen' was, however, further proof that they did things differently in the Hill, which was plagued by shifting sandhills and cursed with some terrible dust storms; there are photographs of some of the worst prominently displayed in town. The Hill was in real danger of being swallowed by its landscape when, back in the 1930s, they did something about it. Horticultural enthusiast Albert Morris convinced the locals and some of the mine managers that if they could keep the rabbits and stock away, the country could come back to life. The 'regen' was born.

It worked, and now forms another barrier between the Hill and 'Out There'.

I was beginning to notice something. When the locals talked about going anywhere, there were only three possible destinations: you either went 'up the river', 'down the river' or 'away'. Up the river from Broken Hill or down the river from Broken Hill—these were places that you knew about and visited. Anywhere else was simply 'away'.

Came the night before the races, and there I stood in the hotel foyer, my recorder primed and ready, waiting along with all those other walking cash points for the bus to take us to the racecourse. I didn't expect to collect any interviews—people would have other things on their mind—but a croupier's call from a roulette table or, better yet, a 'Come in, spinner!' would be great background for the colour picture I'd paint for broadcast on Sunday morning.

He was a very big man and very friendly, but when he told me that there was a man who wanted to talk to me over at the bar, it was pretty obvious that he expected me to go immediately to see the man at the bar. The gentleman in question wasn't wearing his working clothes (they would have sported a fair bit of silver lace) and it turned out that he too was very friendly and concerned for my wellbeing. Obviously, he thought that my recorder was weighing me down and would prevent my having fun, because he took it from my shoulder, handed it to his companion and said, 'You go and have a nice time. We'll mind this for you.'

They look after their own in the Hill.

The races were great. The oysters cooled on beds of green ice. The Guinness flowed, and everyone had an Irish ancestor. Civilised picnics were the order of the day—yes, with crystal glasses—and if you looked a little lost, an immediate invitation to join someone for lunch was on offer. You had no chance of winning fashions on the field without a touch of green about you, and if the winner of the cup wasn't called Shillelagh, it should have been. St Pat would have approved.

I can't tell you about the recovery—I was too busy presenting the program. But before I left the Hill, I had to have John's picture.

'You don't want that.'

'I do, John. I do. I want it very much. Could we come to an arrangement about paying it off?'

'Everyone can paint,' my host insisted. 'You'll like it much more if you paint your own memory of Broken Hill. Go away and paint.'

This really sounds silly: I did try to paint that mullock heap. But John was wrong: not everyone can paint. It's almost fifty years ago, but I still remember *The End of the Tar*.

THE LITHGOW FLASH

IT WAS SUPPOSED TO BE A STRAIGHT-UP-AND-DOWN-THE-MIDDLE SPORTS story. I was interviewing this nice old bloke in Lithgow. He had a stable of young professional runners, and that was the story.

We were sitting on one of those wooden-planks-on-tree-stump seats they have around old sporting fields and showgrounds. This one was at the Lithgow Showground, where he was training his 'stable'. We'd just about finished the interview when he casually mentioned that he'd trained Marjorie Jackson.

Marjorie Jackson? The Lithgow Flash? I once had pretensions to being a runner, but I had neither the talent nor the work ethic. Marjorie was my hero. 'Here? You trained her here, at the showground?'

'Yeah.'

'What was she like?'

'Nice girl.'

It turned out that her parents were a bit doubtful about letting her, a young girl, train with the men—but train she did. In fact, that competition with the men may have stood her in good stead.

'Didn't understand pain, Marjorie,' the old bloke confided.

He told me that he'd thrown everything he could think of at her in one training session, and at the end she'd sat slumped, exhausted, on a seat just like the one we were sitting on. 'Don't sit there, girlie,' he told her. 'You've got to run up that hill before you finish.'

'That hill' is a small mountain that runs up from the back of the showground. Without a word, Marjorie shrugged off the Army greatcoat she was wearing—no tracksuits in those days—and headed off.

Many years later I met the lady herself, and we sat down for an interview. In true fan fashion, I told her that I'd seen her beat the then world champion, Fanny Blankers-Koen, at a meeting in Sydney in 1949, and I could even tell her what she was wearing: a blue singlet with a dark-blue sash. She was impressed.

Then she told me about the trip home afterwards, back to Lithgow.

It was a trip by steam train in those days, and the famous Zig Zag Railway was still in operation. The driver knew who he was carrying home, and as he hit the Zig Zag he started to blow the train's whistle. By the time they pulled up at the station, half of Lithgow was there at the railway to meet her.

'Only half?' I asked.

'The other half was on the train with me.' She was cheeky.

Marjorie was named for Lithgow. Everyone knew her as 'the Lithgow Flash', and in many ways the town owned her. They had a mile of pennies in the main street to fund her trips away; even the kids laid down their pocket money.

The fastest tracks in the world then were cinder tracks. The town didn't have one. Australia didn't have one. The people of Lithgow built their Marjorie her track.

It's history now, of course, but she won gold for us at the 1952 Olympic Games in Helsinki, not once but twice—our first track victories since 1896. Small wonder we loved her.

Gold, gold for Australia? Well, perhaps not.

She recalled waiting to be called to the start in the 100 metres final. The runners were marshalled in a bare concrete room under a grandstand. There was a washbasin against the wall and Marjorie was terribly nervous; she was dry-retching into the basin.

The Lithgow Flash,
Marjorie Jackson. A gold
medal for Mummy and
Daddy and Lithgow.

She remembered the start and she remembered the finish.

'When I crossed the line and knew that I'd won, I looked up and said, "Thank you, God. That's for Mummy and Daddy and Lithgow."'

She wasn't nearly so nervous before the final of the 200 metres, and when she crossed the line victorious on that occasion, she looked up and said, 'Thank you, God. That's for Marjorie.'

THE POSSUM

THIS COUNTRY TOOK EVERYTHING FROM HIM, AND YET HE LIVED OFF this country.

You might call 'the Possum' a hermit, but there was much more to this New Zealand shearer stranded in a hostile country than mere hermit.

Griffith, New South Wales, had a hermit for years. He lived in a cave overlooking the town. He had a little garden and people used to visit him. Not the Possum.

Every town or district has one—the loner who doesn't quite fit in. They're the old bloke or woman you see tramping the road in an overcoat. They're the character who turns up once a month at a small shop to cash their cheque from the government and buy some stores. These days it's fashionable to describe them as 'suffering a mental illness'—not the Possum. In Australian bush lore, he is unique.

Jon Lamb sent me the story from Renmark, South Australia. He had the story from Max Jones, the local detective sergeant, who knew more about the Possum than anyone.

People had seen this little old bloke wandering the river and hadn't been too worried about him. He'd been seen up and down the river, from Renmark to Wentworth, and he'd never caused any trouble. People had gone out to fix a fence they'd known was down, but found that someone had been there before them: a rotted post had been 'dummied' up and the wires tightened. It wasn't the fairies: it was the Possum.

That wasn't good enough for Max Jones. He didn't want anyone wandering his patch who might have questions to answer, and he made it his business to find out who this stranger might be.

Max's diligence paid off. He and the Possum shared a surname: the Possum was New Zealand citizen, David Jones, born in 1901. But what was he doing wandering the South Australian bush almost 70 years later?

David Jones had come to Australia in the late 1920s to work as a shearer, and he had been a good one. But came the Depression and things got tight, work was scarce and David was out of work. That was a disaster. He didn't have the money for his union dues; he didn't have a 'ticket'. No union was tighter than the shearers': no ticket, no work. He couldn't ply his trade.

He wasn't the only one, and there was a remedy of sorts. You could go 'on the track'—wander the bush looking for casual work, supported by track rations, a voucher that you'd pick up at the police station that would get you enough basic food to get you to the next town. You could do that, but not David Jones. He wasn't an Aussie, no track rations for him. So David Jones turned his back on Australia and became the Possum.

When Jon sent me the story, the Possum hadn't tasted bread for almost forty years. He lived in the bush and survived on what the bush could provide. Fish from the Murray of course, and rabbits, feral cats and foxes for meat; for greens, bush tucker he'd learned to collect. And honey—he had a taste for honey and knew how to get it. But there was one thing he needed from society: salt.

People would report the sound of wood being chopped. Investigation would reveal the Possum at work at the family wood pile. He'd finish with a pile of split and stacked firewood, and in the tradition of the bush, he'd get a food parcel. Tea, flour, sugar, salt, bread, some meat, tinned food. Next morning the parcel, minus the salt, would be back beside the pile. The Possum didn't accept charity.

The legend of the Possum grew. People had seen him dressed in a suit coming back from a trip to Adelaide. Police up the river had picked him up, but Max had put the word out that they were to 'leave the Possum alone'. He'd been seen as far down south as the mouth of the river, as far upstream as the Darling in New South Wales. The lock master had seen him in the middle of winter, an oil drum under his arm for support, crossing the Murray with the mist rising off the water. The whole time, in his own quiet way, the Possum was working—he never gave up his responsibilities as a stockman.

In the middle of a drought, people would go out to cut scrub for the sheep, only to find that the Possum had been there before them, breaking down boughs so the sheep could get at them. They'd muster a mob to check for flies and find that a struck sheep had already been cleaned up.

They saw the Possum from time to time. He was a little man, but fit and strong. He was clean, his hair was cut, after a fashion, and he'd shaved somehow or other. He picked up his clothes from the sheds after the shearers had gone—there was always something left behind. He left little caches of 'usefuls'—an axe head, clean clothes—stashed up and down the river.

People might accidentally bump into the Possum out in the bush, but he wasn't interested in conversation. He'd hurry away.

The Possum was an old man when Max Jones uncovered all his story, and Max made it his business to get close to the old man. The thought of him dying alone out there in the bush—or, worse, being trapped, caught by an arm in a tree as he robbed a hive—nagged at Max. He would get him into town. He'd get the Possum a quiet end.

The two men did strike up some sort of relationship. Max even managed to record a conversation he had with the Possum. The old bloke covered his mouth when he spoke, and it was difficult to hear him. He told Max that he regretted losing touch with his family, and worried about his mother.

Max explained that by now he could surely get a pension. Perhaps he should come into town and be checked over by a doctor?

I couldn't understand much of what the Possum had been saying, but his answer to this suggestion came through clearly: 'I'll be alright when I get me ticket. I'll be alright then.'

Max didn't get him into town, and the Possum died as he'd lived some sixty years of his life, alone in the bush. They found his body beside the river in 1982. They've got a statue of him now at Wentworth, where the Darling meets the Murray.

THE DEDICATED WHARFIE

A WHARFIE, FROM THE DAYS WHEN MEN VALUED THEIR ABILITY TO WORK hard and competed with each other in feats of endurance, was prodigiously strong and loved to show off. These were the days when we exported our wheat in bags, and his favourite trick was to carry five at a time.

Yes, I know that a bag of wheat weighs 180 pounds—around 80 kilograms—but this is a bush yarn, so work with me.

His trick was to put one across his shoulders, behind his neck, and pick up two under each arm. Loaded like this, he'd trot up and down the gangplank all day.

Came the day when he slipped and plunged into the harbour. His horrified mates watched as he sank below the oily water, and then fought his way to the surface, only to sink once more. Gamely he struggled back to the surface for the second time, but as we all know, there's no third chance.

Just as it seemed inevitable that he'd sink to his doom, he shouted to his mates: 'If someone doesn't chuck me a rope, I'll have to let go of one of these bags!'

TWO SPLENDID FISH

'YOU'VE GOT A FAN. SOMEONE LEFT THESE FOR YOU.'

'These' proved to be two of the most magnificent fish I'd ever seen. They weren't stuffed and mounted, nor were they alive and swimming in a plastic bag filled with water. They were ready for the pan—and it would need to be a big pan.

The staff of ABC Townsville was gathered around my catch. They explained that I was looking at a red emperor and a coral trout, the finest reef fish you could eat. With them was a note welcoming me to Townsville and wishing me a good program. Already I liked the place. North Queenslanders are a touch paranoid. They think that the rest of us don't give them their dues, and they could be right. Townsville, the unofficial capital of the north—and, as the locals are quick to tell you, the largest city in tropical Australia—was about to put that right.

It was 1970. I was in town for the first Townsville Pacific Festival. Performers were coming from Papua New Guinea, the Philippines and Malaysia. There would be music, theatre, dancing and the Queensland Symphony Orchestra would perform. This festival would mark the city as the cultural capital of the Pacific.

We Australians wouldn't buy *Blue Poles* for another three years, and the Australia Council for the Arts wouldn't be fully funded for another five years. Townsville was really putting it out there. But what to do with two fish?

I met the commander of a patrol boat the Navy had sent as its contribution to the festivities. He seemed to have no one to shake hands with, so I asked him if he could use a fish, and instantly we were friends and I had an invitation for a meal aboard his boat. That accounted for the red emperor.

In the end, I decided to freeze my coral trout. I was told that this was sacrilege—but how else was I going to get it back to Orange? I'd done a careful check of the timetables, and if it came straight out of the freezer and onto the plane and all the flights were on time, my family would be dining on thawed coral trout that night.

This was a big fish, and by the time I'd wrapped it in several layers of insulating newspaper and then bundled the lot in brown paper, I had quite a parcel.

The lady in front of me at the airport was not happy. She was carrying a very young baby, and she was hung about with all the paraphernalia that an infant needs on a plane trip. The inspector was unhelpful. He wanted everything, and I mean everything, out of that bag on her shoulder.

Why mince words? He was an officious bastard who seemed to enjoy being difficult. I mean, how was the woman supposed to nurse a baby *and* empty everything out of her bag? I made a half-hearted offer to help.

No, I couldn't take the articles out of the bag for her, and she certainly wasn't going to let me nurse her baby.

'What's in the parcel?' the inspector asked.

My turn. It was hopeless. I knew that, but you've got to give it a go. 'Ha, you'll never believe it. Someone gave me this fish. It's a beautiful fish. They tell me it's a coral trout. It's frozen, and I've got it wrapped up like this to keep it frozen till I get home.'

Not a flicker of interest. 'Unwrap it.'

With four or five layers peeled away, I reckoned the outline of a fish was unmistakable, and I looked up hopefully—to be met with a basilisk stare. 'More?' I asked.

He didn't even reply. I kept unwrapping till there it was, in all its naked splendour. He didn't say a thing, but just watched while I wrapped it up again.

The people behind me in the queue, meanwhile, considered whether they really needed to fly that day.

GIFT COLLECTION

THERE ARE LEGIONS OF STORIES ABOUT PEOPLE SENDING BIRTHDAY CARDS, wedding gifts and the like to their favourite characters in TV soapies, and after you've been 'on air' for a while, some people do think they know you. Of course, all they really know is the persona you project on air. Hopefully that will be something like the real you—but who knows?

People sent or gave me things, and I hope I had the good grace to be embarrassed. I always wanted to say to the sender that I wasn't the important one in this equation—after all, I wouldn't exist except for the people and the stories that gave *All Ways on Sunday* its character. They were the important ones.

It's not unusual, when you visit a winemaker and do a story, to depart with a bottle of produce. But what if your interviewee mines opals or gemstones? Some of the gifts I received were valuable; on other occasions—which was more embarrassing—they were obviously very valuable to the sender.

Waiting for me at the studio in Launceston on a visit was a brick—a house brick. Its significance was the fact that it was a convict brick from one of the earliest buildings in the state. The thumbprint of the man who'd made it was there, preserved in the brick for as long as it continued to be a brick—but shouldn't it have stayed where it belonged?

In Alice Springs I got a gift that confused me. It was obviously Aboriginal and very old. It looked something like an out-of-shape boomerang, and the note with it told me that it was a 'killing boomerang'. I imagined that it could have been used as a club. It might have been used in hand-to-hand fighting. To me it was a curio, until I decided on a little research.

My gift was a curved kylie. It was old, it was real and someone had once depended on it for food. I held it in my hand and wondered who'd held it for real. Who had made it, and depended on it for hunting? And what gave me the right to 'own' it?

The best I could do was present it in turn to the high school my children were attending. It had a collection of artefacts it used as teaching materials. What else could I do?

THEY'RE OFF!

THE LIGHTNING RIDGE RACETRACK WAS ONE OF THOSE PLACES WHERE the shout 'They're off!' was a signal for a cloud of red dust to rise. Somewhere in that cloud, sundry horses and jockeys were doing their bit to make the bookies rich—but punters had little idea where their fancy sat in the mob until the last couple of hundred yards, when you'd catch a glimpse of the colours through the dust.

The Ridge also had a small group of trees growing on the far side of the track, and I swear that the hoops could have changed horses in that clump of trees and we spectators would have been none the wiser.

I was there, discussing the state of the crops and other important matters with a local, when my twelve-year-old daughter 'tapped' me for two dollars for a bet.

That was paper money at the time. She had her grandfather's blood in her alright. She had a hot tip. She was backing Bogan Jewel.

My companion happened to own said horse, and politely suggested that she put her money somewhere else.

'She's a very pretty horse,' observed my daughter.

'Yes, she is, dear, but she's not going to win this race.'

Her grandfather would have got the 'mail' immediately. But it seems that sort of nous isn't passed along in the genes. My daughter gave the owner a withering 'what would you know?' look.

As my dad would say, 'Experience is the best teacher.'

THE ROCK

'DARWIN ON THE LINE, CALLING ORANGE RECORDER. DARWIN CALLING Orange recorder.'

That was Peter Knudsen, a regular *All Ways on Sunday* reporter. This would be one of the great colour pieces from the Top End that he regularly sent, and it was coming via a landline from the ABC's Darwin studio.

'Roll tape, please. Roll tape.'

I pushed the button and settled back to be entertained.

'Identification,' and there followed a name with very obvious Middle European roots and a title. Peter was talking with the managing director of a Northern Territory mining company, who was worried, very worried.

It was 1973 and It Was Time. We had a new government, hellbent on changing Australia. So strap yourself in and enjoy the ride.

Let's get a little perspective on this. The latest change of government wasn't the political merry-go-round we're now used to. It had been 23 years since the government had changed, and every day brought a fresh announcement from a stable of ministers who'd done a 20-year apprenticeship on the wrong side of the despatch box and were in no mood to tarry.

Peter's interviewee had an 'arrangement'—well, more of 'an understanding'—with the previous government, and was concerned that the new broom would sweep his company away. Remember that the Territory was then controlled from Canberra, and Aboriginal

Land Rights wasn't yet a popular slogan. Australians, by international standards, were still innocents. We weren't yet used to hearing the phrase 'It's in the national interest' trotted out in support of some very doubtful enterprises. But this particular manager's work was certainly in the national interest.

He was mining, or preparing to mine, a rare metal. The world was just starting to understand the true worth of this mineral, and potentially this was Australia's next gold rush. It was as big as that—so long as this new government kept out of the way and let private enterprise get on with the business of making us all rich.

I was perplexed. Why was Peter sending me this story? This was 'hot' news. It should be aimed at *AM*, our flagship current-affairs program.

'Why should the government be concerned?' Peter enquired.

'We're mining in a sensitive area,' responded his guest.

'Where?'

'Ayers Rock.'

'How close to the Rock is the mine?' Peter asked.

'No. No,' came the accented reply. 'The Rock. The Rock.'

Peter tried again for some clarification, while his guest fumbled for the words to make himself understood: 'The Rock. The Rock.'

Then the penny dropped. 'Ayers Rock?' Peter queried. 'You're mining the actual Rock?'

Now he had it. This was just exploratory work, you understand, but his company had been taking core samples from the Rock, and they'd proved to be particularly rich in this rare mineral. They'd been working discreetly with the local Aboriginal people, away from the view of tourists, but of course all that would now have to change.

The business plan to support full-scale mining had been developed; within months, mining activities that would make this country and his company very rich would begin. Surely the new government would see the wisdom of this exercise?

Something was very wrong here. I let Peter's story run a little longer. If any of this was halfway true, it was explosive stuff. Why was he sending it to me?

I spooled the tape back and listened again, carefully. Knudsen had a marvellous facility for adopting voices and accents. He was interviewing himself. The whole story was a 'have'—but, boy, it was a good one. Of course, next Sunday would be April Fool's Day—this was a bit of fun.

I let the story roll, and as it progressed, the story of Peter's 'interviewee' became more and more bizarre. I was worried that he'd take it just too far, but no. The story was certainly nonsense, but there was enough doubt there to make you wonder: could this possibly be true?

I put Peter's story to air on Sunday morning with a completely straight introduction and waited. It didn't take more than five minutes for the phone to ring, and at the other end of the line was a very angry man.

He introduced himself as an assistant to one of our new ministers. He was good. Did I have any idea how irresponsible this sort of action was, he demanded furiously. 'This is the sort of underhanded business this government intends to stamp out.' He wanted names, details, contacts. They'd be putting a stop to this vandalism.

Really it was a tremendously impressive tirade, but I'm not as green as I am cabbage-looking. I wasn't about to be 'April Fooled' over an April Fool's Day story.

'If you could just let me have your phone number, I'll get those details for you,' I promised.

When he did so, I went cold. I'd been working in Parliament House as a political reporter just the year before, and the number he rattled off was horribly familiar. He was working for one of our new ministers.

The great thing about working for the ABC is that you can always depend on the corporation to defend you. I rang Graham White and asked for his advice on dealing with what was proving to be a very embarrassing situation.

His advice was succinct: 'You did it—you fix it.'

A VERY OLD-TIMER

I WAS IN LAUNCESTON TO DO THE PROGRAM, AND MY CONTACT HAD lined up a chance to talk with one of the very old-timers from the Beaconsfield mine.

We have a vision of the diggers being tough individuals, but of course all the really profitable mining was company mining, and those diggers were employed workers. I wanted to know what it had been like working underground for someone else.

It didn't look promising. The 'talent' I was introduced to was certainly an old-timer, but I wondered how much of a grip he had on today. He was wearing an overcoat—but as far as I could make out, that was it. He had stories of the terrible conditions underground, but he was most interested in telling me of the schemes the workers had developed to steal gold.

Early attempts to smuggle gold out in their 'cribs' (the containers they used to carry the food for their meal breaks) weren't at all successful, but the scam that worked best was to secrete gold in the grease around the hubs of the axles of the old wagons and retrieve it later in town. Where there's a will, I guess.

All the heavy machinery for the mine had to be shifted there; I remembered I'd seen a massive piece of rusting equipment. I asked the old-timer how they'd carted it.

'Bullocks,' he assured me. 'You remember when that got here? You remember? It was the day we got the news that Mafeking had been relieved.'

I had to tell him that my memory didn't stretch quite that far back. (Mafeking was a town under siege in the Boer War. Relief came early in May 1900.) Obviously there was nothing wrong with his long-term memory.

ANAKIE

THE MOST EXPENSIVE GIFT I EVER RECEIVED WAS TWO SAPPHIRES, BUT the lady who presented them to me valued them not at all. She hailed from Anakie, Queensland, and she and her husband were changing the way they mined sapphires.

I'd been invited to open the annual show at Emerald, the principal town of the gemfields. I can't say I understand the practice of 'opening' agricultural shows, and I pity the poor society secretaries who, year on year, scour their brains as they try to find someone who'll open next year's show.

I like the job, and I did it in all sorts of places; I met a lot of very interesting people that way. But, as I say, pity the poor secretary.

The Emerald Show gave me a chance to get to the gemfields. That Sunday the program would be broadcast from the ABC's Rockhampton studio, which, they told me, used to be the safe of the old Mount Morgan Gold Mine, and that meant a 340 mile (or 545 kilometre) round trip to get out to Emerald and back. Another job for the poor show secretary to organise.

Anakie was a contradiction. The first miner my guide introduced me to was a young failed farmer. Drought had forced him off his place, and he'd brought much of his farming machinery to the gemfields, modified it and used it to turn what had been a hobby into a business. Indeed, as I was to find, it was a very lucrative business.

Everywhere else on the field I met fossickers, and they all had one thing in common. They all carried a little presentation case containing the very best of the stones they'd found, beautifully cut, polished and presented. Naively, I thought sapphires were blue and that was that. I had a lot to learn.

Nestled in those little cases I saw gems of every colour, from gold to green to black, as well as the traditional blue. And I saw my first and only 'pigeon's blood' ruby. About the size of a split pea, it nestled in a snow-white presentation case and, yes, it did pulse. I'd never seen anything like it.

Gemstones have been part of the history of this area of Queensland for a long, long time. I met an old lady who'd found her first stone at the turn of the century; she was the first to tell me to 'pop the stone in your mouth. A sapphire is hard and cold. You can tell.'

She had been a little girl bringing the cow in to be milked when she spotted a likely looking stone lying on the side of the track. She picked it up and popped it into her mouth in the approved fashion; she got such a shock when it was an emerald that she promptly swallowed it. Mum and Dad did the only sensible thing: they sat her on the pot until it reappeared.

Now, fossicking is about luck, good and bad, and my guide was anxious to show me a photograph depicting the worst luck any group of miners ever had.

His photo was in black and white, and the half-dozen or so sons of the soil depicted had faces set like stone and arms like tree trunks folded across their chests. They were big boys and they were having their photo taken, and that was serious business.

Each had a foot on a bag in the centre, a leather bag about the same size as the one footballers these days use to cart their gear to a game. There was a bit more than boots and jockstraps in that bag—it was full of uncut sapphires. You could only guess at the amount of money in that bag, but it represented a year's work for those young hopefuls.

'Can you see what's wrong?' asked my guide. 'Have a look at the date.'

The photograph was dated May 1914. So?

'The only place in the world that cut sapphires then was Germany,' laughed my mate. 'The poor buggers sent that lot off to Germany just before the start of the First World War. Never saw them again.'

Henry had better luck. Henry was your archetypal fossicker. Of indeterminate age, with long hair and a beard, and skin that only gets that colour and texture from years of being baked, he lived in a shed made from tins of Plume Kerosene that had been beaten flat. Power kerosene used to come in those square-sided tins, and you found them all over the bush. Henry had put an awful lot of them to good use. He had a house, of sorts.

'Show him your stone,' ordered my guide.

Henry wore 'Bombay bloomers', and he obediently plunged his hand down the front. He rummaged for a moment or two, and located a piece of string. Using it, he hauled from the depths a little yellow leather bag. He opened it and dropped into the palm of my hand an uncut green sapphire the size of a matchbox.

Stupidly, I gasped, 'God, how much is that worth?'

Laughter all round as Henry asked, 'How much have you got?'

There was a story to Henry's stone. It was roughly the shape of Queensland—well, you needed a bit of imagination, but roughly—and Henry had decided to approach the then premier, Joh Bjelke-Petersen, to buy it and have it cut as the 'state jewel'.

Joh was having none of it, so Henry had to hang on to his stone. But he couldn't resist showing it to people, with the inevitable result that two young blow-ins stole it from him.

They weren't too bright. They tried to trade the stone for a tank of petrol in town, so—unlike the unfortunates in the photo—Henry got his stone back.

And why, with a stone like that in his pocket, was he living in a tin shed and still fossicking?

'Ah, its mate's gotta be around here somewhere.'

That young farmer turned professional miner lived in a shed too. His was a little more upmarket—it was made from fibro. He was sorting the wheat from the chaff. He challenged me from the other side of a conveyor belt covered in what to me looked like very ordinary stones: 'There's sapphires there. If you can pick one, you can keep it.'

Politeness pushed me to choose a very small sample, and he chided me to be a bit more adventurous. Eventually, I picked a stone that looked a bit different and held it out for inspection.

'Put it in your mouth,' he commanded. 'Go on, put it in your mouth.'

I did what I was told and waited for the magic to happen. Nothing.

'Is it cold?' he queried.

Well, of course it was cool—it was a stone.

'Cold? Really cold?' he insisted.

I confessed it was not.

'That's because it's a lump of blue metal. You can have two more tries.'

So I'm not going to make a fossicker.

Later, I watched as he sat down with a visiting Thai gem buyer. The men sat on opposite sides of an old mirror and spread stones across it. Depending on the way light reflected through the stones, they sorted them into piles; when both were satisfied, they shook hands and the buyer opened an overnight bag stuffed full of big notes and counted out money. This was a cash-and-carry business.

My miner told me that on occasion he'd take a suitcase of uncut stones to Thailand and do the business there. I can only imagine a suitcase of sapphires going through the X-ray scanners now in place at every airport.

While the miner and the buyer were chatting, the young man's wife offered to show me her hobby. She collected 'fancies', she said. Would I like to have a look?

From that fibro shed she brought a four-litre ice-cream container full of carefully washed, rough sapphires of every conceivable colour and shape. She proceeded to give me the layman's tour of the business.

She explained that the mineral which gave the stone its colour wasn't always concentrated all over the crystal, and you could get different, even mixed colours, in a crystal. Then she showed me a long piece of crystal, in which blue melded into green melded into gold.

'That's a hound's tooth,' was her explanation. 'It's the end of the crystal. Oh, look—here's another one.' And she pulled a similar-looking stone from the collection.

There looked to me to be a considerable amount of money in that ice-cream container, and I couldn't help asking the crass question: 'How much is all that worth?'

'Oh, I don't know really. They only want the blue ones. But they are pretty, aren't they? Where are those hound's tooths?'

'I put them back. I put them back,' I assured her.

'Oh, no. They're for your wife, but you must promise me that you'll pay to have them cut and polished. Promise?'

Promise I did, and she gave me the name of a cutter in Emerald. He looked at her/my stones and muttered that 'they may not be anything'. And I left it at that. Later, four beautifully cut and polished parti-coloured sapphires turned up in the post with a bill for cutting.

The irony of all this is that, now that blue sapphires can be synthesised, it's the colours and the parti-colours the buyers want. I hope the miner's wife kept her collection.

Back in Emerald, it was showtime. It was my turn to stand before the crowd, which would obviously rather have been looking at the prize bulls or riding in Sideshow Alley than listening to some boring bloke waffle on. But I declared the show open, and that night the party would be in my motel room. I don't recall organising that—let's say it was spontaneous.

A motley mob turned up, clutching alcohol in many forms, but one among the uninvited guests stood out. This young lady was tall, tanned, terrifyingly fit—and she had a wall-eye. One eye was a pretty blue and the other had that milky-white ring around it. She'd stand out in any crowd.

Behind her back, they told me she'd been running bulls in the Territory. My guess was that she'd been in the business, then popular, of running water buffalo down with a sort of fixed lasso affair attached to the side of a four-wheel drive. If that was the case, she was a tough lady indeed, and worth talking with. It seemed there was an interview there.

In the light of what was to follow, I have to say that I can remember what I was wearing at the time. Remember, it was the 1970s. Rollnecks were all the go, and I'd chosen to wear a black silky-looking rollneck. I know, in the middle of Queensland . . . All I can say in my defence is that we all make mistakes.

I noticed that the young lady in question had been watching me for some time, and eventually she came across to speak to me. Good, I thought: here's a chance to see what she's been doing and line up an interview.

She was direct. 'You a poofter?' she demanded.

'Yes,' I stammered.

Ever since, I've claimed that I said that to make a stand against discrimination. Don't believe me—I was terrified of her.

Her response set me a conundrum. 'Piss this lot off, and I'll take you to bed and fix it for you.'

BREAKFAST AT ALICE

I'D JUST FINISHED BROADCASTING A PROGRAM IN ALICE SPRINGS IN 1974, and as was usually the case when I was away, I'd worked most of the night and had had nothing to eat. I remember wondering aloud on air what might constitute a Territorian breakfast, and I got two very different answers.

Waiting for me outside the studio in the sunlight was an old Aboriginal man with a wicked grin. He clutched half a jam tin of witchetty grubs, which he offered with a sneaky, 'Since you're only a young fella, you can bite the heads off and spit them out.' At least I can say that I tasted them.

Second course came in the form of a 9-gallon keg of beer, complete with the trappings, being wheeled up the path by a local publican. My protest—'We might need a bit of help with that'—was met with a laconic reply: 'Someone'll turn up.' And someone did—Ted Egan with a group of his mates. This was not going to end well.

I'm very well aware of my capabilities, and one look at this crowd of Territorians spelled trouble. I was booked on the first available flight out of the Alice, with connections to get me home to Orange that night, and this group of larrikins was supposed to provide the transport to the airport. It was now about eleven o'clock. Rapid calculations—while I was still able to make them—suggested that, if I was careful, I might just be able to get to that plane in acceptable condition. Let breakfast begin.

One of the group was involved with a CSIRO research project working to ascertain just how much 'pure' dingo remained in the dogs then roaming the Territory. I've always had a soft spot for dogs, so we decamped, trailing the keg, in the direction of the CSIRO research station. I wasn't prepared for what I saw.

Two dogs had just been captured and brought in from the desert, a mature dog and a bitch. They were housed in a long, very securely enclosed run. The roof was, from memory, about seven feet high, and there was a single gate into the enclosure. Now, please don't lecture me on the damage that dogs can do. I've cleaned up my fair share of mauled sheep and shot more than a couple of marauding dogs, but that doesn't mean I can't appreciate a splendid wild animal when I see one.

Here we were: a large, loud, boozy group of humans gazing at two dogs in captivity. The male dog 'set' us. He stood with his hackles up, unflinching. His bitch glided—the only way you could describe her action—up and down the cage behind him, giving a little leap every time she came to the gate. That little leap saw her hit the top of the enclosure effortlessly. There wasn't an ounce of fat on either of them. If you think you've seen dingos in a zoo, then let me tell you: you haven't.

I looked at that dog's eyes. From memory, there were about five of us in the group, but there was not a flicker of fear in those eyes—no sign of him backing down. If we've got one thing wrong in this country, it's our branding of a coward as a dingo.

'Breakfast' might have been having a bit of an effect by this time, and perhaps I waxed a touch lyrical about the dogs, but the suggestion was made that I should have a dingo pup to take home with me. A litter had just been born; it would be no trouble to 'nick' one. For the rest of the day I had to keep checking my pockets for fear that the offer had been made good.

It was about now that Ted approached me with some terrifying news. There was a problem with the airlines: my flight had been cancelled and the next available flight out was at about six that evening. I trust Ted. He was telling the truth, wasn't he?

Simultaneously, it seemed, someone in Alice Springs had decided that our group would by now be in need of a 'smoko', and a fresh keg made its appearance. I was doomed.

They did get me to the plane. But I was in that terrible state of knowing that I was in a deplorable condition and yet being desperate to somehow 'hold myself together'.

My escorts were loud and colourful in their wishes that I might have a safe journey and return quickly, and my fellow passengers were not looking on me with favour. A look at the hostess made it plain that, if I knew what was good for me, I'd sit down and be very quiet for the entire flight.

I might have got away with it, but for the fact that, just before the doors closed, Ted burst into the plane clutching a sixpack—to 'keep you going till you get to Adelaide'. Truly, air hostesses are not paid enough money.

Adelaide was the cold breath of reality. My original flight would have linked with other flights to get me home, but now I was stranded in Adelaide on a Sunday night, with no accommodation and a brain struggling to function through the mists of a prolonged Territorian breakfast. I hope they were satisfied.

CAMEL CUP

LIKE AN ELEPHANT, A CAMEL NEVER FORGETS—AND IF YOU'RE CRUEL TO him, he'll wait his time and he'll kill you. Sali told me that, and he should know. He was one of the last of the old 'Ghan' camel drivers, and what he didn't know about camels wasn't worth knowing.

I met Sali Mohamed in 1974, when I was back in the Alice for the Camel Cup. I thought that the worst a camel could do was spit at you, but far from it. 'They fight with their necks,' Sali explained, 'each trying to force the other to the ground. If they succeed, they throw their legs apart and fall on their victim's head with their fifth foot.'

'Fifth foot?'

'Look at a camel's brisket—that is where he rests. It is as callused as a foot. That's what he will use to kill you.'

I agreed that I'd treat camels with more respect in future, but Sali had a glint in his eye as he told me how to gain forgiveness from your camel. All you needed to do, he explained, was take off your clothes—all your clothes—and pile them in front of your camel. The camel would then proceed with great fury to 'kill' the clothes. When he was finished, you could put the clothes back on and start the relationship all over again. Camels are curious animals.

Sali reminded me that a bale of wool is the shape and weight it is simply because two of them made a balanced load for a camel. Proof, if you needed it, of the place camels once commanded.

Of course, he knew all about the revival of camel racing and was quick to tell me that it was nothing new in the Territory. Camel races had long been part of outback entertainment, with workday teams being commandeered for weekend racing, and of course there was betting on those races. Not by the drivers—they were all Muslim, and the Prophet forbade gambling—but drivers were much in demand as 'advisers'.

'During the week, when they are working, every camel knows its place in the line,' Sali explained. 'Every camel knows its leader, and no camel would ever pass his leader. It is a wise man indeed who is friend to a camel driver at a race meeting.'

I was determined to ride in the Camel Cup that year. I'd never ridden a camel, but I reasoned that if you could ride a horse, it couldn't be too different. All you had to do was get on. Think about it: no movie you've ever seen shows you how to get that camel to kneel down so you can climb aboard.

Sali showed me the trick, and I was convinced that it would put me 'one up' when it came to race day. 'Tap your camel on the near-side front knee and command "*Ooshta*",' he told me.

'*Ooshta*?'

'That's right—*Ooshta*.'

I practised a couple of times with increasing ferocity, until Sali was satisfied. I was on my way to becoming a cameleer.

Nineteen seventy-four was my second trip to present *All Ways on Sunday* in Alice Springs, and there was a welcoming party waiting for me at the airport. The plane landed at about 3.00 p.m.; they delivered me to my lodgings at about eleven o'clock the following morning. A week in the Alice is a feat of endurance.

The revival of camel racing was still in its infancy. Almost by accident the locals had discovered how attractive it was as a tourist spectacle, and they were still refining the event. Noel Fullerton, whose bet with a mate had kicked off the event four years earlier, was operating his camel farm, but things were much less sophisticated than they are now.

We would race at Traeger Park, named for the inventor of the famous pedal wireless, and I was amazed at the crowd jammed into the place. There was even a bookies' ring of sorts.

I was staying with one of the organisers of the event, and while there was initially some concern about letting 'this wireless bloke' have a ride, consent was finally given. Thinking about it, the organisation was risking a lot. It had paid to fly me to the Alice to present the program; I wouldn't be much use to them in a hospital bed with a leg in the air, and I soon learned that was a real possibility.

As with every race meeting, there were plenty of minor races leading up to the feature event. In one, all the riders were town 'personalities', and I watched with some apprehension as, halfway down the straight, one of the riders slipped down the back of his camel and under the feet of the field. They galloped all over him. He got up, and I consoled myself with the thought that camels have soft feet.

I don't know what I expected so far as racing gear went. Yes, I'd seen *Lawrence of Arabia*—but would you really race with your foot sort of hooked around the camel's hump? I was relieved to see that the Alice way was to attach what looked like a standard stock saddle to a frame that fitted over the hump.

I could manage that. Watching the experts in action, I saw that the trick was to lean forward over the hump. Feet back, body forward—that was the way.

Some of the riders had their 'colours', but the best I could manage was a paisley-patterned skivvy. They were all the rage at the time; I'd have loved to have seen one described in a race book.

I'll confess to butterflies as we gathered in the marshalling yards. The clerk of the course was allocating camels to riders, and cautioned me about corners. Corners, he advised, could be tricky. Traeger Park is your traditional circular track, with the field running anticlockwise, and it seems that camels, relatively new to this business of racing, weren't comfortable with corners. They were used to running in a straight line; a couple of them had already tried to scale the fence and escape during a race. Something else to remember.

'Which one's mine?' I demanded, sounding a good deal more confident than I felt.

He considered for a moment and pointed to 'that black one over there'.

He wasn't what I'd call black, but he was huge, and he was held by a little Aboriginal boy, who, I discovered, would be leading him to the starting line. The kid looked to be about ten or twelve years old, and was dwarfed by his charge.

With Sali's advice ringing in my ears, I made a confident show of approaching my mount. I was a bit nonplussed—where were his nose pegs? Control, it seemed, would be a touch less sophisticated, and would come via two rope leads attached to a halter. The kid held one lead and the other dangled.

Okay, now: near-side front knee. I tapped and, in my best commanding tone, called, 'Ooshta!'

My camel stood completely unperturbed.

I tried again, which prompted my young squire to enquire: 'What you say to him, boss?'

I explained that the term 'Ooshta' was used to make a camel kneel for its master . . . Did this boy know nothing?

His reply chilled me: 'Oh, Christ, he can't talk, boss. We only caught him Wednesday.'

Okay. I couldn't believe that, but two assistants now made an appearance with a rope. They wrapped it around the camel's legs, and he obligingly collapsed.

'Get on him quick, boss! Get on him quick!' was the command. So 'boss' scrambled aboard.

Have you ever noticed that a camel rises by lurching? First, the back legs hoist you high in the air, and then, just as you're about to sail forward over the hump, the front legs lift to throw you backwards. The outcome is that you find yourself a long way off the ground and in danger of sliding backwards off the beast.

Equilibrium restored, it suddenly occurred to me that if my camel didn't understand the command to kneel, would he understand the command to stop?

'Just turn him into a fence,' was the laconic reply to my query.

There is something exhilarating about sitting high on a camel. Oh, yes, I embraced the whole romantic image. I put a hand on my hip, looked down at the underlings scurrying about below, and gave myself up to the rhythmic sway of this noble beast. This was fun.

As we padded to the start, I began belatedly to formulate a race plan. I'd noticed that earlier fall, and didn't intend to have camels, soft-footed or not, walk over me. I would 'miss the jump'. Pity about that, but, after all, I was just a blow-in from down south. I'd hang about at the back of the field, out of harm's way. I'd finish last and give everyone a laugh.

I lined up on the extreme outside, and it suddenly occurred to me that I had only one lead in my hand. My squire still held the other firm. When would the transfer take place? Someone shouted 'Go!' and I got the answer—the kid threw the lead up in the air and bolted.

God is good: I caught it. Otherwise, we'd have raced around Traeger Park with a lead swinging. I hate to think.

I hadn't communicated my race plan to my mount. He sprang forward as though shot and—shit! shit! shit! We were leading the field! I could have touched the crowds on the fence, and they could have touched me. One did try to hand me a cold stubby—it was a familiar figure. Jimmy Hereen would never see you go thirsty.

Frantically, I tried to remember 'body forward, legs back', and without thinking, I was suddenly taking my weight on my knees and moving in unison with a camel that could run. And could he run! This was exciting.

I'd settled down to enjoy things when the corner into the straight loomed. We were still on the outside fence and he clearly had freedom in his sights. Despite my tugging, his head turned right and I expected at any moment to be joining that mob on the fence in a tangle of camel neck and legs.

I leaned out and began to flog the poor beast across his nose in an attempt to turn his head, the whole time tracing his ancestry back to the sands of Saudi Arabia. And I can assure you none of his ancestors had been married. The thought 'This is terribly cruel' crossed my mind, and I was already mentally undressing to assuage my beast's anger when we crossed the line.

I remembered the advice I'd received in the mounting yard and turned him into the fence to stop. This was good. I wanted to go back and do it again.

I rejoined my host and event organiser in the grandstand with the other official guests. He grinned and asked if I could recall the names I'd called that poor beast on the turn.

I replied that I'd been 'a bit busy at the time and couldn't remember'.

'Ask anyone in Traeger Park—they'll tell you,' he laughed.

There goes Aunty's reputation.

'1974 Alice Springs Camel Cup Tourist Promotion Invitation Race Won by Alex Nicol.' That's what it says on the pewter. I'm a cameleer.

A NEAR THING

LONG AFTER I'D COME HOME FROM THE ALICE, I GOT A LETTER FROM Jimmy. He wanted to keep in touch and tell me of his latest disaster, when he'd been camping out.

'It was a beautiful night,' he wrote. 'I was at peace with the world. Just before I settled down I opened the tucker box and pulled out a fresh bottle of rum. I knocked the scab off, poured meself a pannikin and settled down to enjoy it. I pushed the cork back in and set the bottle down on top of the tucker box right beside me teeth and climbed into me swag.'

That night, it seems, Jimmy broke one of his cardinal rules and camped in a creek bed. He woke up to the sound of the creek coming down.

'Jesus it was close,' went the letter. 'I just had time to grab the essentials and get clear. I lost me swag and me tucker box . . . I get me new teeth next week.

'Your mate, Jimmy.'

THE GREAT AUSTRALIAN
FUNNY BONE

AUSTRALIANS HAVE A UNIQUE SENSE OF HUMOUR. IN 1500 WORDS OR MORE, discuss.

This is a question I'd like to see put every year to final-year high-school students. The examples used to support the arguments would provide a great running history of comedy in Australia.

Some of what we find funny now would shock our grandparents, and likewise some cartoons from their era would be viewed askance today, but a good joke—like good wine—gets better and better. So what is the Aussie sense of humour?

Right up into the 1990s, the manufacturer of Minties ran a series of cartoon advertisements under the banner 'It's Moments Like These You Need Minties'. A classic showed two construction workers who'd fallen from a high-rise site. One clings to an exposed beam. His mate has slipped down his legs, pulling his pants around his ankles as he does so, and is hanging onto his boots, helpless with laughter. The original was drawn in the 1920s, with the caption: 'For gorsake stop laughing, this is serious.' Some things last.

I ran a competition on *All Ways on Sunday* to find Australia's best bush yarn. You could either send your written yarn and trust me to do it justice, or record it yourself on a cassette tape. There'd be no prize, and the audience would be the judge. They rolled in. The best, of course, were those who'd recorded their own yarn. The old adage held good: 'It's not the story, it's the way you tell it.'

Aunty got wind of the competition and decided that a definitive television search for just what made us laugh was in order. John Woods, a young television director, would direct and the search would be far and wide, from the outback to the waterfront, from bushie to wharfie. Of course, the professionals would be plumbed for a contribution—the cartoonists, comedians and actors who make a living out of making us laugh would show us how.

This would be big. This would be *A Long-distance Search for the Great Australian Funny Bone*. My role was to scout for the bush comedians, to coax a story out of the non-professionals, and to sort of meld the show together.

John believed it was particularly important to tap into the wharfie sense of humour—surely that would be a prime example of what tickled the working class. And we'd been told of just the bloke to fill the bill.

It wasn't easy to get onto a wharf, even in the 1970s, but we weren't expecting the last hurdle: the union rep with an enormously inflated idea of his importance. Yes, he knew the individual we were looking for. Yes, he might be persuaded to talk to us, but first: would we be interested in the story of the great progress the union had made for the Australian working man?

'Not really' obviously wasn't the answer that would unlock the wharf gate. This was where I came in.

'Interview him,' said John. 'I'll set up for the shot, but we won't put any film in the camera. Give him ten minutes, a quarter of an hour—that should satisfy him.'

Imagine, if you will, this picture. A group of men stand on the Australian waterfront. Two of them face each other, obviously deep in conversation. Grouped around them are four others, fascinated by what the couple are saying. One holds a reflector to focus the sun's rays on them. To the side, a camera operator films the scene, and beside him a tall sound-recordist holds a microphone boom carefully out of shot to catch their every word, while the fourth man, the director, ensures the artistic integrity of the moment.

Each member of the team solemnly goes about his business, knowing that, although the camera turns over and the sound recorder whirrs, there's neither film in the camera nor tape in the recorder. They're in search of the Aussie sense of humour.

We did eventually find the chosen wharfie, and I mentioned how we'd encountered his union rep.

'Yeah, we call him "the Pill", mate.'

'The Pill?'

'No conception, mate. No conception.'

This time there was film in the camera.

THE SEARCH GOES ON . . .

OUR SEARCH FOR THE GREAT AUSTRALIAN FUNNY BONE TOOK US ALL over the Central West of New South Wales in search of one particular tale teller. He was legendary—we heard stories of him in pub after pub—but we could never manage to track him down. At last a group of blokes outside a pub in Nyngan gave us specific directions to his property.

The mud map they provided was very detailed, and it took a good hour and many gate-openings to get there.

'There' turned out to be the most run-down place I've ever seen. Wrecked cars and rusting, broken farm machinery were scattered everywhere, and a dozen rib-showing dogs barked and howled at us from the end of chains.

This bloke had better be funny.

He wasn't. He did everything but present the shotgun as he ordered us off, but I bet those blokes back at the Nyngan pub were laughing.

Bush humour safely in the can, it was time to tickle the sophisticated end of the Australian Funny Bone. On Sydney's North Shore, a select band was gathered around a pool. Now for some witty conversation—or perhaps not.

Stan Cross—creator of the famous 'For gorsake stop laughing, this is serious' cartoon—took one look at my dinner jacket and offered: 'Flash as a rat with a gold tooth.'

Ray Barrett, just back in the country and a television star now, reckoned that no one could laugh at themselves quite like an Aussie, and he'd picked up a great yarn from a Japanese POW to prove it.

Laughter in Changi?

Oh, yes. This bloke had a routine that turned a sadistic ritual into slapstick comedy.

Some guards, it seemed, took particular pleasure in humiliating big men. The bigger and stronger the man, the more complete his humiliation when you broke him, and they had a ritual, an irresistible challenge to a man's self-esteem, that no one could master.

Pick the biggest and the strongest from the line-up. Kneel him on a bamboo rod in front of his friends, and order him to pick up a rock, a big rock, and hold it arms at full extent right over his head.

Now wait.

Watch his arms twitch, sway backwards, forwards.

Be ready.

Smack those knuckles with a cane. Bring that rock back above his head.

What's worse—the agony in his knees, where the bamboo rod is pressing, the cramping in his arms as they struggle against the weight, or the confusion in his mind, knowing that the rock must fall and with it his manhood?

Giggle like a child when the rock crashes down.

Ray's mate thought this was bullshit. The rock's gonna fall, isn't it?

He marched out. Knelt down. Picked up the rock and held it above his head and immediately dropped the bloody thing. The boys pissed themselves laughing, and even the guards saw the funny side. They didn't try that one again.

Ruth Cracknell was a guest. She had the magical ability of exposing the vulnerability of any character she played. She only had to hold her head a certain way to make you smile. She'd give us a little gem of a performance. While the crew set up for an interview, my job was to get an idea of the story she'd spin for us—except she wouldn't give it up.

Ruth was taking this search for the Australian Funny Bone seriously. No, she wouldn't perform, she said, but she would deconstruct this humour business. James Thurber, the man who conjured up 'The Secret Life of Walter Mitty', was her hero. She'd explain to us how he built his whimsical stories.

'That's fascinating . . . but perhaps a funny story and a dissertation?' It's amazing what can finish up lost in the editing booth . . .

No, Thurber it would be.

Good actors don't like performing off the cuff—they like to have time to craft a performance. I thought that might be influencing Miss Cracknell. 'Perhaps if you had a little time . . .?'

She didn't need a little time, thank you; she was well versed in Thurber's work.

Our star performer wasn't going to perform on cue. This wasn't funny.

'So, she won't tell us a story?' our director asked me.

'No,' I had to reply. 'I've tried everything. We're going to get a lecture on James Thurber.'

A quick consultation revealed that we had about twelve minutes of film in the camera. If Ruth was going to perform, we'd load a fresh reel, but as it was . . . well, we'd shoot off the twelve minutes of Thurber and leave it at that.

The great lady and I settled down opposite each other, my mind racing to think up some halfway intelligent questions to get us through the next twelve minutes.

The clapper marked the take, and I said something like, 'Miss Cracknell, "The Secret Life of Walter Mitty" is one of the great short sto—' that's about as far as I got.

Ruth leaned to within a couple of inches of my face, and turned on a howling, tears-streaming-down-your-face performance. Minute

Ruth Cracknell in full flight. Next question?

by minute she piled laugh on laugh, and all I could think was: *There's only twelve minutes in the camera!*

I treasure a still shot from that interview. My face says it all. I quite literally couldn't speak. Perhaps the secret to this comedy business is the unexpected.

RUSTY

We chanced on Rusty—or, I should say, the late Rusty's owner—in Shindy's Inn, out on the Darling. In what was evidently a very much extended wake, the old bloke was extolling the virtues of this great dog to anyone who would listen. Rusty, if you believed him, was peerless in working sheep, nosing pigs or just plain fighting.

'Ah, 'e wasn't big. Was he?'

The bloke behind the bar nodded agreement. He'd obviously heard all this before.

'But by Christ 'e could fight, couldn't he?'

Another nod.

'He'd sit beside me here and you wouldn't get another dog in the bar. Didn't matter how big they were, 'e wouldn't let 'em near me. Game as a pissant.'

The fact that a television crew was hanging on his every word inspired the old bloke to fresh heights. We were treated to the time when Rusty had single-handedly taken on a huge boar.

'Musta been 200 pounds or more. I tried callin' 'im off, but there's no stoppin' 'im. Rusty's inta that pig like a chicken into hot mash. Pig slashes 'im right down the side, tore the poor little bugger up something cruel, but he kept comin'. There's blood everywhere. The pig's squeal'n and Rusty gets a hold of him by the snout. Well, pig starts throwin' his head around, see, tryin' to shake Rusty loose, but he's got his jaws clamped tight—and once he's got his jaws set, nothin's gonna move 'im.

'Yeah, well, I shot the big bastard, and then we had to get a screwdriver between Rusty's jaws to prise 'em loose. He wouldn't let go.

'Poor little bugger. He's cut up bad, but this isn't the first time I seen 'im like this and I know what to do. I cut a bit of wire outa the fence and I twitch them cuts together—you know, stitchin' 'im up, like. He licks me hand when I'm finished 'cause he knows I'm look'n' after 'im. Doesn't 'e?

'Mad little bugger—I miss 'im. Always in a blue. Gawd knows how much wire he had in 'im at the end.'

He took a long sip of his beer and paused thoughtfully.

'Never really died, y'know. Just rusted from the inside out.'

MILITARY CONFLICT

THE ARMY WAS COMING TO 2CR COUNTRY. AT LEAST, THAT WAS THE promise—or the threat, depending on your point of view.

The proposal was to acquire land in the Orange and Cobar areas. At Orange, land would be compulsorily acquired for a permanent military establishment. At Cobar, the land would be used for occasional military exercises; landholders could stay and work the property and be paid a rent.

The community split. How would we manage the situation?

A local journalist's responsibilities in such a situation are clear. You should provide as much clear and accurate information as is possible, and stay out of the emotive politics. We tried and we failed.

Arguments pro and con became increasingly emotional. There were those, particularly around Orange, who wanted to argue the benefits that a permanent military establishment would bring. All those guaranteed fortnightly pay cheques would underpin the local economy nicely, and then there would be the effect on land prices, as new families moved in.

On the other hand, land which had been in the same family for generations would be compulsorily acquired, and those landholders aired increasingly generous estimates of the productive potential of that land. Their claims were backed by those who argued that those fine Australian soldiers, lauded for their exploits at the local war memorial every Anzac Day, would suddenly become a risk to every young woman walking the streets alone at night.

The local council entered the fray, and the mayor was physically threatened. The situation became nasty, the more so because no one knew exactly what compensation was being proposed.

As the then local ABC manager, I'd been trying for weeks to gain access to the relevant government minister and get some clarification, but could get no further than his press secretary and the message that 'the department is in consultation with the community'.

Each side lobbied the local member and bombarded the station's newsroom with press releases. The protagonists had learned the value of using the media to influence the community. Surely the local ABC radio, which had always been 'their' voice, wouldn't disappoint them now. But it did. We reported the facts and nothing but the facts as they came to hand, and left it at that.

Perhaps twenty or even ten years earlier that would have been that, but changing technology brought changing opportunities. There were television current-affairs programs now crying out for good colour stories, and there's nothing quite like community conflict to sell a show. Heat, not light—that's what sells a story. City television stations would be interested, and indeed they were. The battle got primetime viewing. The bush had learned how to use the media.

I eventually made contact with the minister. 'It was time,' he said, 'that the community knew exactly what was proposed.' I agreed. 'After consultation with the community, we've decided to drop the proposal.'

OLD MICK

'I DON'T THINK YOU KNOW WHAT YOU'RE TALKING ABOUT.'

Now there's a first for talkback radio. The subject was gambling, and here was someone telling *me* I didn't know what I was talking about. Two things my father drummed into me when I was growing up: 'Never run down stairs carrying a pair of scissors' and 'Never bet on an odds-on favourite'.

The caller's name was Mick. He invited me to call him 'Old Mick'. He was of my father's generation and he had a fund of stories. I couldn't get to see him quickly enough.

Mick lived in a tiny town right on the outskirts of 2CR country, and I was surprised he was a listener. He lived alone, and his front room was a cliché: an open fireplace and on the mantlepiece a carton of cigarettes with several packets missing, a half-bottle of Vat 69 whisky, and a photo of Phar Lap with Jim Pike in the saddle.

My father used to stand in front of that very photograph and tell me earnestly that he'd never seen the great horse gallop: 'Didn't have to. He won everything in a canter.'

Mick was a little man. He'd once been a dapper man, but he obviously wasn't well and he didn't belong here in a little country town. Mick was an endangered species. He shouldn't have existed away from the sights and smells of Randwick or Flemington.

My credentials established, we set about the business of swapping stories. Of course he'd been an SP bookie; he'd done time for it when the traditional backhander—'Five quid on the winner of the

Old Mick's Randwick in the 1930s, when racing was the sport of kings.

last'—proved insufficient for the local police sergeant. That had happened more than once, and he was finished with the business now. He was about buggered. He told me he didn't think he had 'long to go'.

I'd offer one of my father's old racing stories, and he'd immediately top it with one of his own, and the more he talked the more animated he became. He told me stories of the 'hoops' (the jockeys) and the ingenious places they'd concealed batteries to make their whips more effective. And then there was the wonderful story of the Red Cross Sting.

Back in the 1930s, a well-known racing identity bet one of the biggest bookies of the day that he could pick six out of the seven winners at a Randwick meeting. The bet was for a considerable amount of money; as a sweetener, the punter said that if he won he'd donate half the winnings to the Red Cross. The bookie accepted the bet and replied in kind. If he won, he too would donate half the winnings to the Red Cross.

Sydney was abuzz. Came the day and a suitably attired Red Cross nurse took station alongside the bookie's stand. She held a sealed box, into which, before each race, and in front of the assembled crowd, the punter placed his selection. The box would be opened after the running of the last race, and either the punter or the bookie would pay up.

The punter picked the card: he correctly selected the winner of every race. And he repeated the scam in Melbourne, where he missed by one and only selected the required six out of seven winners.

Thinking it through, it's ridiculously easy. Before the first race, the punter simply slipped his selection for the last race into the box. Thereafter, all he had to do was post the winner of each race in turn. Get the Red Cross involved and it had to be on the square, right?

Old Mick was a great storyteller. I wanted him as a regular contributor, but he lived a long way out from the studio and I couldn't keep coming back.

THE AUCTIONEER

THE ABC 'POWERS THAT BE' NEVER COULD UNDERSTAND THE VALUE OF livestock market reports, and it was a constant battle to keep them on air in the morning.

'Boring' and 'off-putting' were the popular phrases used to denigrate the service. Mind you, the batting and bowling figures for Sheffield Shield matches or the daily call of the Sydney Stock Exchange were a completely different kettle of fish. They were vital information.

I have to admit that 'A slightly increased yarding of plainer types saw values remain firm' didn't yield a lot of useful information, but if you got a report from a stock and station agent who had a sense of theatre, the business really came to life.

I can remember one who'd report along the lines of 'little droughty lambs . . . you know the sort, Nic—you could pick up three under each arm. They sold at . . .' The same individual could, with perfect logic, equate the rising price of old bulls in the marketplace with the progression of the football season and the consumption of meat pies.

At Orange we were very lucky when a young stock and station agent, David Williams, started up his own business. He'd report the local stock market 'live' in the studio, and he took his responsibilities very seriously.

In an attempt to make a feature of the market reports, I decided I'd record various auctioneers in action and use these sound effects to introduce the service. Each agent would get a turn, and the listeners could have fun trying to pick whose technique was the best.

I mentioned to David that I hadn't recorded him in action yet, and he invited me to the saleyard that very day. 'I'm going to break the record for the highest price paid for a beast in the yards,' he claimed with great confidence. 'Get that on tape.'

David was in great form. He stood on the rail extolling the virtues of the biggest bullock I've ever seen. Four hundred dollars rapidly became $450; then $460, and all the while the excitement grew. Bid after bid he collected from a group of buyers keen to make their mark on saleyard history.

I forget what the target price was—let's say $600. As the bids mounted, more and more people crowded the fence. And all of this was on tape.

The magic figure was reached and passed.

'Are you done? Done? All done? Sold!'

The exultant buyer collected a round of applause and the congratulations of his colleagues.

Later, I suggested to David that he'd been a bit cheeky nominating that he would break the saleyard record. He could have finished with egg on his face.

'You don't know the half of it,' he replied. 'I didn't have a bid until I got to $540.'

Now, that's theatre.

THE MILKY BAR FAIRY

She dubbed herself 'the Milky Bar Fairy', and for a price would visit your newborn in hospital and bless the child with a shower of Milky Bars. You could even have a souvenir photo of the event. She challenged me that I would not have the guts to give her a job as a freelance. Challenge accepted.

Andree Withey came back with a story from a local inventor. It will surprise you to know that all these years you've been using the 'throne' in the smallest room in the house incorrectly. That's what's been causing everything from arthritis to earache, but it's not your fault. The 'throne' is wrongly designed, and Andree's inventor had the answer.

You can't draw a set of plans in an interview, but his description of how the job should be done left little doubt that his services would have been keenly sought by the interrogators of the Spanish Inquisition.

Andree was on a roll. Her next mission? 'I'm going on a parachute jump and I'll describe what it's like from the time I leave the aircraft to the time I hit the ground.'

Robert Peach, who then controlled all the ABC regional stations, remarked that he'd 'spent the war trying very hard not to have to do what the young lady is planning'. He strongly advised against it.

Andree's description of the descent was riveting. She clearly loved the sensation and enjoyed describing it. Unfortunately, she was so engrossed in telling us about it that she'd forgotten that at the end of every jump is the ground, and she was unprepared for its arrival.

As they loaded her into the ambulance with a fractured pelvis, she started to describe the trip to the hospital. What a trooper!

At this time, Radio National had a program called *Practicalities*. In essence, it was about inventions and how to use them. Hospital proved a fertile ground for Andree, and the producers were offered stories on everything from how to use a commode to why shy young men chose a private ward—clearly the sound of urine hitting the end of the 'bottle' was too embarrassing.

She was incorrigible.

THE RIGHT THING

I ALWAYS THOUGHT OF 2CR AS FAMILY. I KNOW ALL THE STAFF DID, AND I'm sure many, many listeners felt the same way about the old girl. Why? Principally, I suppose, because we knew that we could depend on each other—presenters, journalists and listeners—and together we'd 'do the right thing'.

Doing the right thing sounds terribly dull these days when 'fake news' is so fashionable, but doing the right thing could have very practical consequences.

We had a wanted man on the loose in our country. He was one of those clever bushmen, and he'd led the police a merry dance for months. Of course he'd become a media celebrity—the city newspapers and television stations couldn't get enough of him.

At this stage I was managing the station, and Amos Bennett, our senior journalist, gave me the news that one of our listeners had just rung to tell us the wanted man was in her chook house. She told us first.

Of course, he'd told her to ring the police, and they were on the way. But it was ten minutes to news time and Amos had a scoop. 'Nic, we know he has a radio. If I run the news, chances are he'll make a break.'

'What do you want to do?' I asked.

'We'll hold off till they've got him.'

Amos lost his scoop, but I reckoned he'd done the right thing— and that that philosophy would eventually land us a bigger scoop.

BEST ON SHOW

The president of the Walgett Jockey Club was a bit embarrassed when he rang. They were another of the country tracks anxious to tap into the tourist market, and the big event this year was the Black & White Cup, sponsored by the distributors of Black & White Whisky. There'd be a 'Fashions on the Field' contest, and the sponsor had been invited to be the judge.

But there was a problem. Saturday was the big day; it was now Wednesday, and there'd been no reply to the invitation.

'I know it's very late, but would there be any chance . . . ?'

Nothing like knowing you're the second choice.

My wife, Diana, had her eye on a very stylish Spanish white hat that would go a treat with her navy outfit and was very keen. A day at the races. A night away from the kids!

In Walgett, Fashions on the Field was a discreet affair. None of this calling out the contestants to parade in front of the mob. Diana and I would wander through the crowd during the day and quietly select the best-dressed lady and gentleman. Very proper.

We'd made our decision just before the feature race, and were in the committee rooms giving the good news to the president, when a beefy bloke clad in stubbies, thongs and T-shirt introduced himself as the Black & White rep. He'd been looking the fillies over, he said. Then, tapping Diana on the shoulder, he announced 'this little lady' as the winner.

I'm not sure how we got out of that one.

THE DOC

'I REALLY WANT TO BE A SPORTS JOURNALIST.'

'Of course you do—you and 40,000 others,' was my first thought. Half the kids who've played school rep football or cricket and can name the last five grand final winners imagine themselves as a gift to sports broadcasting. If only they knew.

The young bloke in front of me certainly wasn't straight out of school. I put him in his late 20s, early 30s. He looked like a real-estate salesman but he wanted to be a sports reporter.

2CR always welcomed triers, but I told him that I had no budget for a freelance and could not offer him a job.

No matter—he wanted to learn.

If he could find a story, I offered, I'd teach him how to write a script and how to conduct an interview. Who knows? We might even get to tape editing. But understand: no job. Deal done.

I'll say this: he was a quick learner, and the station's sports coverage blossomed as a result. Within a couple of weeks he was working on his own and starting to pile up neatly packaged sports stories, ready for broadcast.

There was only one problem: he never seemed to leave the place. Look around and there he'd be: sportscoat draped over the back of a chair, tie neatly knotted, spinning the reels of a tape editing recorder like a professional. He was a natural. He had a good eye for a story and knew instinctively how to pick an interesting angle, and people obviously liked him.

Enough is enough. 'This is becoming offensive,' I told him.

'What?' Naturally, he was upset and I had to explain.

'I told you I had no money to pay you and couldn't offer you a job. You're turning out good, valuable material, and I can't keep taking your work without paying you. It's not right. It's offensive.'

'I don't mind.'

'I do. Look, you're always here. Your own job must be suffering, and your boss, whoever that is, can't be too happy.'

He grinned and said, 'Don't worry about it. I'm on a house call.'

'House call?'

'I'm a doctor.'

Doc was in fact a young local GP, and he cordially hated his job. People, he told me, came into his rooms with the flu, the mumps, depression or whatever. They sat on one side of a desk; he sat on the other side. Before they left, they had passed across that desk to him whatever infection they'd brought in. He couldn't stand it anymore. He wanted to be a sports reporter.

'But all that training,' I argued. 'Those years of training. Perhaps sports medicine?'

'No. Sports reporting. This is fun.'

He left Orange after a couple of months, and took with him a 'show reel' of stories to impress any editor. His name popped up years later as a by-line on the back page of *The Sun*, Sydney's afternoon paper. Doc had become a sports reporter.

Seeing his by-line prompted the memory of a story he'd once told me of a time when sport and medicine had collided fortuitously for one of his patients. The man was in the midst of a massive heart attack, and Doc needed to know, and quickly, how long he'd been in pain.

'Can you tell me when the pain started?' Doc demanded.

'When Border got out,' came the gasping reply.

'I knew to the second,' Doc said.

THE DOGGER

THE DOGGER REMAINS A MYSTERY. FOR A START, HIS CRAFT WAS PART black magic, or at least a hangover from a time past. His business was killing dogs, and it made him quiet and reserved to the point of self-effacement. Everything about him—his clothes and his manner—was designed to make you forget him. The success of his business—and he was very successful—depended on his being next-to-invisible. He didn't smoke (unusual for a bushman) because 'the smell hangs around'.

To emphasise something when he spoke, he'd point with his chin. His hands were still.

He spent hours, days and sometimes weeks alone. He was content with his own company and not easy to interview. A testament to the success of his strategy is the fact that I honestly can't remember where I met him.

I think I won him over because of my love of dogs. I always had a good dog when I was working stock, and as a townie I've always had a pet to spoil. We had some common ground.

He squatted as he told me some of the tricks of his trade. It was the typical bushman's sit-on-a-heel squat. He liked to be close to the ground, and he was comfortable. I wasn't. I was cramped, but once he started talking I didn't dare move for fear of interrupting him.

He had been paid to kill dogs all over Australia, and yet he told me how much he admired dogs. 'Better than humans' was his summation. He told me that once, when he was hunting dogs in the desert country, he'd come across dozens of tracks circling an old disused mine shaft. That puzzled him. A closer look revealed a half-grown pup caught on a ledge about six feet down. As far as he could make out, his mob had been feeding him. You have to admire that.

The dogger had worked at a time when the old serrated-jaw gin-traps were still legal; to him, setting one was a work of art. It was vital that there should be no trace of him, no sign or smell that a human had had anything to do with the trap, because that would give the game away. As bait, he used a trick. He took a small bottle out of his pocket and held it out for me to smell—and you didn't have to get very close to get the pungent whiff. It was urine taken from a bitch in season. He carried that bottle with him everywhere, and just a couple of drops in the right place all but guaranteed he'd have a dog in his trap.

And dogs are clever. 'You get one chance at a dog,' he said. 'If you miss that chance, he won't forget you and you'll never get an easy shot at him again.'

He told me the story of his hunt for a particularly clever bitch. That story left me wondering how he felt about his kill.

He'd been hired to clean out the dogs on, I think, a place in Queensland, and he'd been successful. But one old dog—he was pretty sure it was a bitch—had beaten him. 'Oh, she'd come across men before,' he reckoned, 'she knew their tricks and she wasn't having anything to do with them.'

He debated leaving her, but he had a reputation to maintain, so he pulled a trick out of the bag. 'I decided I'd paper her in. You know, catch her with the *Sydney Morning Herald*.' He chuckled.

No, I didn't know how you could 'paper a dog in' with a newspaper.

'Well, she's afraid of humans,' he started. 'She'll run a mile to get away from anything she thinks humans have had anything to do with. So you use that against her.' And he spun me this story of incredible patience and cunning.

The idea was to take a newspaper and to tear it into strips. The place was big, but he reckoned he knew which paddock she was in. So he walked that paddock, twisting a strip of paper into every panel of fence. He left a couple, which were screened by some trees, free. Then he got a jackeroo from the place to drive to the back of the paddock and 'beat' towards those panels he'd left free, while he settled down to wait.

He'd been chasing this bitch over the past couple of weeks, so he'd got to know her. He respected her. She was a cunning old girl.

He picked up his first sight of her as she made a bolt for the fence. She spotted the paper flapping there and, just as he predicted, she backed away.

He spotted her again as she tried in a different spot, with the same result. Of course she found the panels he'd left free, and he let her come to him and then shot her cleanly.

'Oh, she was a clever old girl, that one,' was all he said.

A RUSH OF BLOOD

WHAT WERE THEY THINKING? IT WAS LUNACY. IN AN AGE WHEN THE business world is all about corporate image, and when logos and corporate colours are zealously guarded, the 'powers that be' at the ABC's head office decided to allocate a small amount of money to each regional station to be spent on 'promotion'.

They decided to allow—to encourage—individual regions to express their own personalities. What madness was this?

At a meeting of minds, we at 2CR reckoned that 'I'm Proud to Own 2CR' sounded just right. We'd encourage every one of our listeners to take ownership of the place. But what would be our logo? Aunty's 'pregnant worm' was nowhere near sexy enough.

My elder son, who had a talent for drawing comics when he should have been doing homework, overheard our discussions and came up with an image of an old man emu at full stretch carrying a tape recorder, and with a microphone attached to his neck and swinging in the breeze. He captioned it 'We cover the country'. Genius. That was us.

Now, how could we get the message out there? Memory tells me that our advertising—sorry, promotions—budget was absurdly small, about $200. Another meeting of minds thought that the best thing was for us to do a 'loaves and fishes' and multiply it. We would have the logo and catchphrase screen-printed on T-shirts. We'd sell them, and as the money came in, we'd print more T-shirts, and so on, ad infinitum. What could possibly go wrong?

The great T-shirt sale: rank
commercialism at the ABC.

The T-shirts were a phenomenal success and the money flowed in. Naturally, we had to open a bank account to handle this business we'd established. And, just as naturally, the auditor was not impressed when he came across an ABC bank account controlled by a couple of enthusiasts from the bush.

Involuntary liquidation swiftly followed. But I still have my T-shirt.

THE DEMO SATELLITE DISH

IT WAS 1985 AND SATELLITES WERE FLYING AROUND UP THERE, AND WE were at the cutting edge of using them to transmit radio and television. The federal government had introduced the Homestead and Community Broadcast Satellite Service. Each homestead or isolated community could buy one of these systems, and it would bring first-class radio reception—and, more importantly, television reception—to outback Australia.

The demonstration model was set up at 2CR. At the heart of the system was a receiving dish. It was very much like the dishes you now see set up to receive cable television, except that it was about 6 feet (2 metres) in diameter.

You carefully pointed this dish in the right direction, and it collected the satellite signal and concentrated it into a tube positioned over the centre of the disc. There the technical bits took over and converted the concentrated signal into TV or radio. That was the theory—except it wasn't working.

A bevy of heavies from Sydney was standing around the wretched thing and checking again and again this or that connection with complicated-looking instruments. No signal was getting through, and no one could put a finger on the cause.

Of course our PMG techs had been interested onlookers. They were working with similar equipment up on Mount Canobolas, where the satellite was going to do magical things for telephone connections.

One of our old techs had been watching the proceedings carefully. Finally, he pulled a biro from his top pocket, leaned in and pushed it up the tube where the signal would be concentrated. When he pulled it out, the remains of a spider and its web coated his pen. And we had a signal.

Later on, winter and the snow on top of Canobolas proved a problem. Snow in the satellite dishes there distorted the signal. Heads were scratched, and measurements taken for specially constructed fibreglass domes to be fitted to the dishes.

The old techs went into town and bought one of those covers you place over a kid's round swimming pool. That did the trick.

THE RIDGE

'PLEASE DON'T BROADCAST THE RAINFALL FIGURES.'

The request came from Lightning Ridge, the opal-mining town out in the north-west of New South Wales. *Don't broadcast the rainfall figures?* Things were changing out there.

I first got to see Lightning Ridge in the 1960s. It was still an opal-mining town. People were living in caravans and lean-tos, and the famous bottle house wasn't quite finished. If you've never seen it, I can tell you it's an example of someone's quiet genius. They built a house entirely out of mud, with bottles—all sorts of bottles—embedded in the mud. That's bush insulation at its best.

People were still drifting in to mine opals, and it wasn't polite to ask where they'd been before they turned up at 'the Ridge'. There wasn't much in the way of storefronts, and Harold Hodge had just bought the trams that he was going to turn into motel units. Harold had introduced his now-famous opal false teeth and loved to tell the story of how he wore them when he met the Queen. What she thought when she saw that smile we can only guess at.

You could, and people did, 'noodle' (put your head down and scramble through the mullock heap that someone had left at the head of a mine shaft, looking for a bit of colour), but it was politic to ask for permission before you ventured onto someone's claim. There were mine shafts everywhere and it was dangerous to wander about after dark. Disputes weren't settled by dropping someone down a shaft, but people did fall into them. And opals were bought by a handful of people working in the Ridge.

And the rainfall? It was very important. Water was always short in the Ridge.

Please don't broadcast the rainfall figures. What was going on?

While I never saw the Ridge before it was a raw mining camp, I did get a glimpse into what that country must have been like back then. I had an invitation from the owner of the homestead block of one of the original runs. He wanted me to see how they'd once lived. I wasn't ready for what he showed me. I should have been, but I'd never thought of Australia the way he showed it to me.

The room was long, dark and cool, and a table ran down the centre. How many would it seat? I can't remember now, but perhaps ten, maybe a dozen down each side. The table was covered with glass, and under the glass were some beautiful silk Indian shawls.

'The jackeroos sat here,' he told me. 'And they dressed for dinner.'

You really needed to walk outside and look about for a minute to comprehend that statement. I was there in a drought year. The country was that hard red-yellow colour, with a smudge of olive green provided by the tough plants that were hanging on. If you looked at the ground you saw pebbles, and under them the soil. Then the heat hit you. It didn't just come up from the ground; it closed in from all around you—and it was dry, so dry. Nothing was going to get done in a hurry out here.

'They dressed for dinner?'

'Absolutely. They were young gentlemen.'

I mumbled something about it being a bit hot for a collar and tie, and my host showed me the fan that cooled the room. It was a beautiful brass fan—it might have come from any expensive retro-furniture store—but they didn't have electricity back then, did they, so how . . . ?

He showed me the mechanism. It was virtually a little spirit lamp burning methylated spirts to make the fan blades spin. Heat producing a cooling draught—like the room itself, the whole thing was a contradiction.

'Do you like the floor?' he asked me.

Because the room was dark, all I could see was that the floor wasn't made from floorboards. It looked like polished concrete, but that couldn't be right.

'It's dung,' he told me. 'Stamped dung, and it got that polish by being swept and swept and swept by the black girls who'd have worked here.'

It occurred to me that I might be getting a glimpse of the colonial India that I'd read about in my *Boys' Own Adventure* annuals. But this was Australia. Of course it must have been like that, but why hadn't we heard our own stories of this sort of thing?

I'd been a jackeroo. I know what I learned from a very good master. He taught me some things about myself that I found uncomfortable, and like every good teacher, he gave me some principles by which to lead a life. Who were the jackeroos who sat around this table? Who was their master and what did he teach them?

Browse through the history of the old race clubs, cricket clubs and what have you of colonial Australia and you'll bump into some famous names. Charles Dickens' sons were sent here to learn to be men. Many of the young blokes who sat around tables like this one, and who dressed for dinner, had no qualifications other than that they were the sons of Victorian English gentlemen, sent to the colony to make their fortune. You've got to ask yourself: did they make the country, or did the country make them?

I walked out into the light that hurt, and the heat.

Please don't broadcast the rainfall figures. Why?

That request had come to me during the late 1980s, and the Ridge was now very different. I'd met Herman 'The Shark' Kreller, opal buyer and character, who'd set up business in the main street. He proudly displayed the 'Shark' pejorative as part of the name of his business.

'People come here expecting to be ripped off when they buy an opal,' he told me. 'I don't rip anyone off, but they're tourists. It's part of the fun to say they've bought an opal from the Shark.'

The Ridge was changing. You could get a cappuccino and a counter lunch. Accommodation, including the now famous tram motel, was good, and people didn't bother so much with noodling—they bought a piece of potch from the Shark. Tourism was all the go.

There was a water supply—not enough, mind you, but a supply. But this was black-soil country, and the road into town was still dirt. If people thought they might get bogged while heading for the Ridge, they would bypass the turnoff.

Please don't broadcast the rainfall figures.

BROADCASTING
ON THE MOVE

For a very long time I'd had a secret desire to have an outside broadcast unit—a caravan or some such that we could take to important events around our region and broadcast 'live' from.

I'd broadcast 'live' from the first National Field Day, that now famous comparative exhibition of farm machinery and knowhow, when it moved to its permanent site at Borenore, just out of Orange. That involved me sitting on top of the office roof clutching a microphone and listening to what was happening back in the studio via an earpiece connected to a portable radio. Not ideal.

But a portable studio was wishful thinking, of course. Such things cost money. Aunty had them in the capital cities—but for a region? Forget it.

'You know, if we could get a caravan, I think we could build a portable studio.' This was a tech talking, an old hand. He was with another tech, a very cluey young bloke on the way up. The young bloke, it was explained to me, needed to complete some practical examinations to get his next grading. This could be done by going through the charade of setting up dummy bits and pieces in the workshop, or he could do something practical—he could build a portable studio.

'But the gear,' I argued. 'The microphones, turntables . . . I'll never get a budget to buy that sort of gear.'

It seemed that, like my Irish granny, these techs never threw anything out. When they replaced a turntable or a microphone or the like from the studio with a newer model, they stored the old one away. 'It might come in handy one day . . .' Well, that day had arrived.

'It'll be old-fashioned gear,' they warned. 'But it'll do the job.'

We did find an old-fashioned plywood caravan that was still registered, and those techs patiently stripped it bare and turned it into our own outside broadcast studio. It was hell to tow anywhere, but we loved it.

A PUNCHY INTERVIEW

Young boxer Spike Cheney was our local hope for the 1988 Olympic Games. A Lithgow boy, he took the adage 'Never stand if you can sit, never sit if you can lie' to the edge. I've never met a more relaxed athlete—until you put him in the ring. There he wouldn't stop hitting you—very quickly, and very hard.

We had a new freelance journalist operating in Lithgow. We wanted to build our audience in the coal city, and he wanted to go on to bigger and better things. The perfect match. He rang to ask if we'd like an interview with Spike.

Everyone was doing an interview with Spike, he was told. Do something different, he was told. He did.

He strapped his small recorder to his body, taped the microphone to his chest, pulled on the gloves and stepped into the ring with Spike.

I got to edit the result. I heard a question being asked; then the unmistakable sound of a glove hitting flesh; then a cry of pain; then a muffled 'Sorry' from Spike, before he gave his answer to the question. This sequence would repeat and repeat.

As editor, my only dilemma was: how many of our intrepid reporter's cries of pain should I leave in? It was the funniest thing I've ever heard.

RAIN AND POWER

Silk stockings and chocolates were keys to the Kidman empire. Sir Sidney (not Nicole) Kidman was known as the Cattle King of Australia. As a boy, he famously rode out on a one-eyed horse with £5 in his pocket; at his peak, he owned or controlled anywhere between 85,000 and 107,000 square miles (221,000 and 277,000 square kilometres) of country from the Gulf of Carpentaria to South Australia. He made his money following the rain.

Those chocolates and stockings went to telephonists in tiny post offices all over the back country. When it rained, every station manager in the outback sent a telegram to head office recording how much had fallen. Kidman's gifts came in exchange for a copy of those telegrams delivered to his office, and meant that he knew more about the weather than anyone else at any time until we got satellite technology There's money in knowing when and where it's rained.

I gleaned that titbit from a senior CSIRO scientist who was working to 'prove' the colour of the salt in Lake Eyre against satellite images as part of the developing science of weather forecasting. Apparently, Lake Eyre is one of the brightest white spots you can see on our planet from space, and colour plays an important role in the interpretation of satellite images. He told me that, at the time he was working at the lake, the satellite picked up a curious stain on the lake. 'It looked,' he told me, 'as if someone had spilled a glass of port wine over grandmother's snowy white tablecloth.'

That had to be investigated. The stain proved to be a huge cloud of plague locusts, half a kilometre wide and several kilometres long, which had picked up a weather front that had petered out over the lake. There they were, a great smorgasbord of pickled grasshoppers on the lake surface. Weather is the stuff of life or death.

Drought brings the dark side, of course, and I once visited a woman living in the Western Division of New South Wales whose life was centred around sweeping the never-ending drifts of red dust from her home and listening to the weather forecasts on the radio. She could pick up South Australian stations, and her day was spent tuning from station to station, chasing the reports of fronts moving across the country. One of them must bring rain. I can only imagine the torment she felt listening day after day after day and hearing that there was no hope of relief.

Autumn rain was generally the excuse for a great outpouring of joy at 2CR. All planned programs would be shelved, and the phone would ring constantly as listener after listener reported: 'Half an inch at Tullamore', 'Forty points at Mudgee', 'an inch at Wellington', and so on and so on. Everyone was anxious to share the good news, and within a quarter of an hour you'd have a great picture of where the rain had fallen and how much it meant to so many people.

You could fiddle with whatever you liked on the program, but the advice was 'Don't touch the weather forecasts'. But of course you had to be part of the action, and every self-respecting rural reporter had his or her own rain gauge, so you could add your tuppence worth.

I had proudly reported a healthy total in my gauge one morning, when the phone rang and a very proper voice at the other end enquired as to whether I had a young son.

I assured my listener that indeed I did.

'He's been using your rain gauge for an improper purpose,' was his retort.

It may be that because broadcasters are so associated with such life-and-death information, some listeners accord you a status you have no right to. We were in the middle of a locust plague, and facetiously one morning I suggested that there'd be money to be made in setting up a company to put up a huge net and trap the nasties. They could then be ground down and turned into sheep feed pellets. After all, they'd eaten so much of the sheep feed that it would be poetic justice to see them fed back to the sheep. After I'd said this, cash turned up—sometimes considerable amounts—to buy shares in the company I'd proposed. Tell me—the idea wouldn't work, would it?

Worse was to come one day when I was informed by a researcher from the Department of Agriculture that such and such a farmer would be worth talking to. This farmer had sunk a considerable amount of effort and money into a new and, to date, untried crop. 'He must know something I don't,' suggested the researcher. 'Give him a bell.'

The famer in question was delighted to hear from me. He drove me with considerable pride to the paddock containing the crop, and I set up the recorder on the bonnet of the car so that we could look out over what was a pretty impressive crop of linseed. My first question was: 'Tell me, what decided you to try linseed?'

This was met by an awkward silence, and then: 'You suggested it on air.'

The arrival of futures contracts on the farming scene produced a unique problem. How to explain the concept of selling the promise of delivering some goods sometime in the future that you had no intention of ever delivering, and then afterwards buying back your promise? Futures trading is now part and parcel of every successful producer's marketing strategy, but there was a time when growers depended on the average price for fair average-quality wheat pooled from all over Australia, or the guaranteed cushion of support provided by the floor price of wool. Futures trading was then something akin to black magic. It was notional nonsense, but it was the future, and I struggled to explain it to my listeners.

'You haven't the faintest idea of what you're talking about, have you?' I'd been trying to explain the concept of the just-introduced prime lamb futures contract, and that was a pretty brutal, but accurate, summation of my efforts. It came from a listener who was one of the new breed of bankers selling this product. 'You'll never understand it until you've had the experience of selling and buying a contract,' he said.

'But I don't have any lambs.'

'And you don't need any. That's the point.'

This savvy listener took me in hand. I'd sell a contract and he'd track that contract for me each week. He'd cover the cost of the contract, and if we made any money, we'd donate it to a charity.

It worked. He'd pop into the studio with a breezy 'You owe me such-and-such for a call.' And then he'd proceed to explain on air the business of keeping the contract alive. His visit became a must-hear segment.

I either knew more about the market than I thought, or I was just lucky, but when I came to buy my contract back, we had made some money. I was obviously good at this business.

Shortly after, I was stopped in the street by someone I'd never met. 'I've got a lazy $6000 play money,' he said. 'Would you play this futures market for me?'

Because it excites your imagination, I think radio is, or was, the most powerful broadcast medium. Listeners form an image of you based entirely on the sound of your voice. 'You' exist in their mind, and depending on the mind involved, that produces some odd results.

'You' can take on the persona of wise sage, matinee idol or the Antichrist.

Neil Inall was balding as a young man long before the look became fashionable. I remember as a young trainee trailing him to a property, where he was greeted by the wife of the establishment with a disappointed, 'Oh, you're Neil Inall—and I shower with you every morning.'

THE BLUEY

THE MAN WAS A GENIUS, A MARKETING GENIUS. HE TOOK A COAT, A BOWL and a calendar, he put them together in his shop window, and people from all over the city went out of their way every day to look at them. They talked about that coat and that bowl at work. They bet money on what was going on in that window, and it was the subject of sweepstakes in offices everywhere. People followed this annual event with all the intensity of Test cricket scores. It was as exciting as watching paint dry—and that was the point.

The city was Launceston, and I had a freelance reporter there with an eye for the quirky and a love of history. His story on the bluey hit the bullseye on both counts.

My mother would have approved of the bluey. Those of us of a certain age remember a childhood when for half your life the sleeves of your 'good' clothes hung down to your knuckles, and then for the other half they rode up three inches above your wrist. Clothes were meant to last, and they did. Mothers had an 'eye': they'd pick up an inferior garment, feel the cloth and toss it aside with a dismissive 'You could shoot peas through it'.

But not the bluey. They say that the bluey descended from the ugly, shapeless, locally made coat that clad the convicts of Van Diemen's Land, and even in its later manifestations the bluey belonged to the workers. If the provision of a bluey wasn't part of the award conditions for Tasmanian wharfies, the union wasn't doing its job. This dull, blue/grey waist-length work coat was guaranteed to keep you warm and dry, and our marketing genius could prove it.

Each year, at the beginning of winter, he would suspend a new bluey from the ceiling of his shop window. Threads held up the body of the coat so as to form a shallow dish, and then he filled that dish with water. Under the bluey he set the bowl, and beside it the calendar.

Each day another day was crossed off that calendar, and the people of Launceston took bets on when the first drop of water would soak through the bluey and drop into the bowl below. Genius.

PRESIDENT BUSH

DEVINA, OUR RECEPTIONIST, WAS IN TROUBLE. HER MESSAGE WAS: 'Come—quick!'

These days all ABC studios are protected, after a fashion, by a security door and a keypad. But back then anyone could, and sometimes did, wander into the studio for a chat while you were on air. Not this time. Devina was defending the studio from a very angry visitor.

I rushed in to be confronted by a very big man making incoherent threats. I cajoled; Devina rang the police; he left.

The police were very cheerful. They knew him well. He was a patient at the nearby Bloomfield Mental Hospital, and was usually 'gentle as a lamb, quiet as a mouse, harmless'. Chocolate set him off, they explained. He'd march into a supermarket, pick up a dozen or so large blocks and stalk out, leaving a string of protesting checkout girls in his wake.

He'd eat the lot. Then he was trouble. We'd simply got him on a chocolate day.

'Well, he threatened our receptionist,' I answered, 'and I want something done about it.'

'Love to, mate,' came the breezy reply. 'Look, he's a patient from Bloomfield. We know him and he's generally no trouble. Now, if he actually hit you . . .'

Yes, well that prospect was not inviting. Our friend was a big, powerfully built man in his mid-40s. Personal hygiene wasn't a priority. He had a tangled mass of black hair, and when he was angry, as we'd seen him, his face was almost as black as his hair. He wasn't going to hit me if I could avoid it.

'Nic, he's back!' Devina was obviously frightened this time, and I wasn't much better.

I tried to reason with him. 'Why us? What do you want?'

He made it clear in short order that we were fools—worse, traitors—and that our actions in thwarting him would have serious consequences. 'I need,' he glared, 'to talk with President Bush on a matter of national importance.'

Where's a policeman when you need one? Devina was sidling away, and my task was clearly to calm him and get him to leave.

My response—'President Bush is a busy man and we may not be able to make contact'—was swatted furiously aside. He shouted that I was deliberately trying to prevent him from passing on vital information, and he became more and more agitated. Obviously, one wrong move now and our cheerful cop would get his wish and be able to pin an assault charge on him.

I tried again. 'Perhaps if you told me . . . if I interviewed you, for example, I could pass the information on as soon as I can make contact.'

That really set him off. What sort of clearance did I have? How did he know that I could be trusted? This was just a ruse to prise information from him.

There were still no signs of flashing lights or the friendly sound of sirens. Desperate times call for desperate measures. I took him into a 'dead studio'. There was no chance that he could go to air, but he could speak into a microphone and see dials move.

I put a fresh tape on the recorder and set it in motion. Tape was spooling. The VU meter was fluctuating encouragingly. He was in touch with President Bush. I closed the studio door.

Devina had made contact with the boys in blue. They were busy on another call at present, but would be around as soon as . . . etc. Great.

Fifteen minutes later, our agitated friend emerged from the studio a changed man. He was calm. He seemed rational. The president, I was informed, was 'grateful for my assistance and asked that his thanks be passed on'. I was suitably impressed. Then he warned me that the tape must be guarded with my life.

'Straight into the studio safe,' I assured him. He insisted on shaking hands. He thanked me again and walked calmly away. I erased the tape.

When the police came, I told them that we'd been able to talk him down, but that it had been scary.

'Told you, mate. Gentle as a lamb. Wouldn't hurt a fly. Good as gold.'

The next week he came back. We repeated the pantomime, and when he left, I played the tape back. You never know—James Bond resorted to all sorts of subterfuge to get messages back to M. But it was gibberish. Unless our learned friend was conversing in code, President Bush could sleep soundly.

He came back again. I won't say we were enjoying it, but we were no longer in fear of our guest. We'd learned the secret: you calmed him by allowing him to speak into a microphone for fifteen minutes, and he went away satisfied. It was a nuisance, but he was no longer a nuisance to anyone else. We were performing a public service.

The next time he came back, I went to arrange his studio—but, no, this time was different. Those tapes, the ones he'd recorded, he must have them. Now!

The old signs of mounting anger were back. He paced. He became agitated. I swear I could smell his anger, or perhaps it was my fear. The tapes, of course, were long gone, erased as soon as he'd finished his 'broadcast'.

'They're not here,' I began. That wasn't the right answer, and now he was really angry. 'I just didn't feel they were safe.' I was making this up as I went along. 'I sent them to head office for safekeeping.'

And it worked. He slowed. 'To Sydney?' he demanded.

'To Sydney. You understand . . . top-secret stuff like that . . . junior officer like me.' Oh, I laid it on.

'And they got there safely?'

'We sent them by courier in a sealed envelope.'

I was convincing. He calmed. He actually congratulated me on my foresight, and we exchanged the now requisite formal handshake of co-conspirators and he left.

I vowed never again. Gentle as a lamb or not, something had to be done about him. But, for now at least, problem solved.

Two days later, the ABC's managing director, David Hill, wanted to talk to me. He had a very big, very smelly, very angry man in his office demanding some tapes. Would I like to explain?

Sometimes you can be too clever.

ON THE OUTER

I KNEW I'D DONE IT—I'D COMMITTED A FAUX PAS IN THE PUB. BUT WHAT did I do?

'Two beers, please,' I had said.

That seemed a reasonable request. It was well after opening time. It was hot. We'd been working. Why the glare from the barman?

The beers hit the counter.

I passed one to my helper, who'd turned up unasked to lend a hand as we were unloading camera and recording gear into the pub. Nice bloke—chatty, friendly. A bit diffident about accepting my invitation to have a beer, but here he was.

Then it hit me. He's an alky. It's a small town. Everyone knows he's having a battle to stay off it, and I'd just dragged him into the pub and put a beer in his hand.

He wasn't chatty now; I couldn't get a word out of him. He downed the beer and shuffled out.

'Don't bring him in here again. He's barred.' The barman was not happy.

What do you do in that situation? Apologise? Ask what he'd done? Shut up?

'Sorry. Didn't know.'

'He won't be round here long.'

There was no one else in the bar, and it was obvious the barman was desperate to tell me the story. My helper was the local cop.

'You barred the local cop?'

It turned out there'd been a big fundraiser the previous weekend. Gymkhana out on the claypan. Raising money for the bush nurse. Things are tight—the drought. No one's got any money but . . . the bush nurse, you know.

'He never put his hand in his kick all day. Got pissed. We locked him in the back of his paddy wagon and left him there.'

The locals had taken the law into their own hands. They'd left him in his own paddy wagon overnight on the claypan. He'd had to sit there and listen while they cleaned up after the big day.

It was summer. It's a wonder that he was alive when they let him out.

The barman was right that the local cop wouldn't be around much longer. Either he'd apply for a transfer, or a word to the wise back in Dubbo would see him moved. You need to be a diplomat to enforce the law in a small community.

THE TIMES THEY ARE A-CHANGIN'

Sir William Gunn will address a meeting at Walgett. It's the late 1960s. Once-mighty wool is on the slide. This talk of a floor price scheme is dividing the graziers, and the great man—at this time the chairman of the Australian Wool Board—is making one appearance only. The meeting will be a beauty. It has to be covered.

Orange to Walgett is over 400 kilometres by road, so it's a case of me finishing my breakfast session and driving to Walgett. Attending the meeting. Interviewing Sir William. Driving back to Orange. Editing the material and writing the story. Then putting it to air the next morning. A long day, but exciting.

The world is turning over. Mother England is joining something called the Common Market. The days of an Australian pound for a pound of wool are long gone. Country that has never before seen a plough is now going over to wheat. Stock water is being eyed for its irrigation potential. Farming consortia are planning mini irrigation districts in country that has only ever grazed cattle. Mysterious explosions sometimes destroy those new banks that are being constructed so as to divert water. There are stories everywhere. It's a great time to be a journalist in the bush.

But there was a price to be paid. A once-hungry world was awash with food. Australian farms were producing too much wheat, and they had only one buyer, the Australian Wheat Board. Its response was to regulate who could deliver wheat to them and how much they could deliver. Johnny-come-lately growers could make their own arrangements.

The young man from Nyngan was angry, and I was his target. He'd sold his sheep—the mob that his father and his grandfather had so carefully bred. He'd bought a tractor, a plough and trucks; he'd learned to grow wheat, and now he couldn't sell it. He depended on his ABC—on me—to warn him about a world that was changing too fast for him to keep up with. I'd failed him. He didn't know whether he could hold onto the family farm. How did I feel now?

My job came with responsibilities.

In the 1960s, Australian farmers had been represented by a plethora of organisations. In New South Wales the main groups had been the Graziers' Association and the United Farmers and Woolgrowers' Association (UFWA). If you attended a meeting to discuss any one of the dozens of issues facing farmers back then, you'd find the graziers sitting on one side of the hall and the UFWA members on the other side. The trick for any journalist was not to sit at a press table, but to take a seat down the back with the grumblers. That's where you heard what the mob thought. That's where you picked up the good copy.

Would-be rural leaders quickly learned that in a changing world they needed to speak with a unified voice and to learn to use the media. Some were good at it; others were shaky, but unafraid to ask for help. Yes, they'd ask a journalist for help in how to 'get across' in an interview, and the best of them were quick learners

This new generation of farm leaders, these agri-politicians, brought about a change in our relationship with our audience. The cosy 'We're All Part of the One Family' approach was gone. The rules were changing. We journos needed to treat these people as professional politicians and give them the respect they deserved, or we'd pay the price.

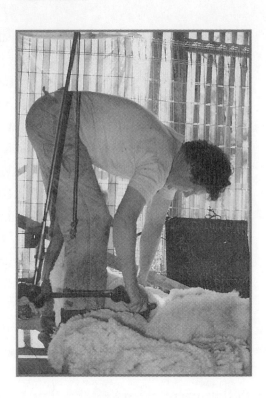

Bending the back. The things
you do to get a story.

There was no issue to better illustrate the change than the wide comb dispute in the early 1980s.

In a nutshell, Kiwi shearers had traditionally used a shearing handpiece with a slightly wider comb than their Australian counterparts. It made great sense. Most sheep 'across the ditch' were crossbred, plainer-bodied sheep than the Australian merino, and therefore easier to shear.

When there was a shortage of shearers in Australia, the Kiwis filled the gap. They brought their wide combs with them and discovered merinos weren't so hard to shear after all. With their wide combs, they could get through more sheep in a day than the Aussies—and so the call went out from the union to ban the wide combs.

Why? Think of the staff in a shearing shed as a triangle, with the shearer at the apex. The number of sheep he can shear in a day will decide how many shed hands are employed. If he can shear more sheep with new technology, then either the graziers should employ more shed hands or they should pay the same number more money to work harder. That was the union's logic.

If you know your Australian history, you'll remember that both the Australian Labor Party and the White Australia policy grew out of the great shearers' strike of the late nineteenth century, when shearing sheds were burned and armed troops were used to control the strikers. We still sing a song about a bloke who 'jumped into the billabong'. The bush was divided at that time, and now the wide comb dispute was dividing it again.

Woolgrowers and shearers were part of the 2CR family. The dispute raged bitterly over the station's broadcast area. Our job came with responsibilities—including the responsibility to cover both sides of the story.

I went and listened at farmers' meetings and at AWU meetings. I've got to say that the more colourful copy came from AWU leaders. 'My members,' one rep told me, 'will stick like shit to a blanket, and you can quote me.' He knew what he was doing. Both sides knew what they were about. I was a tool to be used.

That dispute grew very nasty. Each side sent me invitations to be present at the next 'spontaneous' outbreak of violence so that I could see for myself what thugs those graziers/shearers were. Better yet, could I bring a television crew? Things got very ugly, and I remember remarking to one particularly agitated individual that, unlike on TV, when you shoot someone in real life, they tend not to get up again.

The age of innocence was long gone.

LET'S DRINK TO THE
NEXT MAN TO DIE

I MET MANY 'CELEBRITIES' DURING MY TIME AS A JOURNALIST, AND FEW left a lasting impression. The drive was always to talk with 'real' people.

In the late 1980s I received a brief that matched perfectly. I was asked to provide the 'pilot' for a special project for the Australian War Memorial. It aimed to tell the stories of ordinary people—the 'real' people I so enjoyed talking with—and how they performed in extraordinary circumstances, in this case the Second World War.

This gave me the opportunity to talk with Philip Opas. In many ways he was, in 1936, an ordinary young Australian. Ten years later he was anything but. He began his military career as a sergeant in the RAAF. He rose to the rank of air commodore, and subsequently enjoyed a distinguished career as a barrister.

The story he told me began as the story of a boy living in an Australia that most of us now wouldn't recognise. His life was shaped by his experiences during a terrible war, and by an extraordinary metamorphosis that brought those experiences full circle.

It was a story that spanned some 45 years, and in many ways paralleled the changes that have happened in Australia.

His story could well have been titled *Innocence Lost and Recovered*.

Philip Opas had a vivid memory of the night the Second World War was declared. He painted a picture of a then sleepy Australia.

On a Sunday night, 3 September 1939, he and his younger brother rushed excitedly into the city of Melbourne to join what he estimated were 'a hundred thousand people wandering around'.

'I'm not sure what we expected,' he remembered. 'Perhaps for bombing to start that night.'

The two brothers joined a curious crowd that walked down to the German consulate; they were disappointed to find it dark and closed up.

Both tried unsuccessfully to join the armed services the next day. There must have been 100 different reasons young men and women volunteered for the forces at the outbreak of the war, but few could have had the insight of the eighteen-year-old Philip Opas. He was studying Law, and International Relations was a crucial element in his course. He had read *Mein Kampf*, Hitler's manifesto, and for some time he had felt it was inevitable that Australia would go to war.

Why?

'Because England would be involved, and if England was involved, it would be unthinkable for Australia not to be involved,' he told me.

He was a fourth-generation Australian—yet he remembered his mother and father, who had never been outside Australia, referring to England as 'home'. He confessed that when, as a young law clerk, he attended the Supreme Court to hear the chief justice formally announce the death of King George V, he had cried. 'I felt I'd lost a grandfather figure,' he recalled.

Philip had obviously been a well-educated and thoughtful young man. But he told me that, until that time, he had never met a foreigner and never heard a foreign word spoken; in that, he would not have been exceptional. Australia, as he was to find to his cost, was a sleepy, ill-prepared outpost.

Before this time, he'd had training with the 46th Infantry Battalion in Melbourne, a militia battalion training volunteers, but now when he tried to enlist he found the battalion headquarters locked up. A couple of days later, when the adjutant made an appearance, he was told, 'We're not actually sure we're at war yet.'

Fed up with waiting, Philip and his brother joined the RAAF. Eighteen months later, when he was well and truly in action in New Guinea, he received a stiff note from the 46th Infantry Battalion's headquarters asking him to show cause why he should not be fined £5 for not attending training.

Philip and his brother both became air crew. One of them flew in the Battle of Britain, and eventually died somewhere in the Western Desert; the other flew against the Japanese in the Pacific, and counted himself very lucky to survive the war.

I was surprised when Philip told me that he'd done his training with the RAAF in New Guinea. It was there he acquired his navigation and gunnery skills. In the early days of the war, he flew reconnaissance missions, searching for submarines ahead of troop convoys. Even then, he remembered an air of unreality about the whole business.

Australia's first air defences in the area were four Qantas Short Sunderland flying boats requisitioned by the government and equipped with First World War–era machine guns. Wives were allowed to join their husbands, and Philip remembered his early days in New Guinea as 'a wonderful fifteen months honeymoon'.

But Australia was about to pay a heavy price for our unpreparedness. In 1941 our modern aircraft arrived: Catalina flying boats and Wirraway fighters. Even at that stage, the Wirraway was obsolete. There is only one recorded incident of it having a victory over a Japanese Zero fighter.

As a sergeant, Philip flew on the new Catalina flying boat—which he described as 'a sardine tin with a crew of eight, 2000 pounds of bombs and 1000 gallons of fuel. A beautiful aircraft when used for the purpose it was intended. It was great at recognisance and at mine-laying, but when we had to carry out a masthead attack on ships armed with anti-aircraft guns, we were a lumbering sitting duck.'

Trying to put his experiences into sporting parlance, I suggested to Philip that it sounded like a second-grade team playing in first grade.

'Third,' he told me. 'Third. We were third-grade.'

I asked what every one of us who had never been tested, as he and his mates were, must wonder: how did you get into that aircraft every morning, knowing the probability was that you would be killed that day?

He began by saying things like, 'When you're young, you believe you're invincible.' He talked about 'whistling in the dark' and making sure that you 'never got really close to anyone, because the blokes you had breakfast with mightn't be there at lunchtime'. And then he sang me a ditty he'd sung in the mess:

> *Stand by your glasses, steady*
> *This world is a world of lies*
> *The best men are dead already*
> *Let's drink to the next man to die.*

'We'd belt that out, banging our glasses on the bar. Goebbels would have been proud of us,' he admitted.

I felt the hair on the back of my neck rise as he said it.

Philip rose through the ranks of the RAAF, eventually commanding his own base; like many who served in that war, he developed a hatred for his enemy. 'I hated them with an unreasonable loathing' is the way he described it. And he saw things that fuelled that hatred.

As a relatively senior officer, he was present when some of the Japanese prisoners of war were released. He recalled seeing a party of Dutch nuns, each of them with their own small child, the consequence of rape.

Following the Japanese retreat at Balikpapan, he came face to face with the evidence of atrocities. There was a personal element to his animosity when he learned that Bill Newton, a ruckman with whom he'd played in the Old Melburnians football team, had been beheaded for refusing to trample on the Union Jack. 'It would have made no difference to the outcome of the war if he had. It wasn't even his flag,' Philip mused. 'But it meant a lot to Bill.'

Perhaps because of his legal training, Philip became involved with the war crimes trials. He witnessed the hanging of three Japanese officers, and delivered to trial Colonel Suga, the commandant of the Kuching prison camp, who was accused of crucifying two women and leaving them to bleed to death over a couple of days. 'I volunteered for his firing squad,' Philip said.

At war's end, he described himself as 'half-mad'. He vowed never to take orders from anyone ever again, and contemplated life somewhere in the bush, away from everything. His wife encouraged him back to the bar, and slowly, like so many ex-servicemen and women, he rejoined society.

Philip Opas had been a keen athlete. 'Above average, but never a champion' was how he described himself. Back in Australia after the war he was active in sports administration, and this brought about what he described as his metamorphosis.

In 1956 Melbourne hosted the Olympic Games, and Philip managed the pre-Games athletic training for a number of countries for a month. Among those athletes was the Japanese contingent. He told me that he approached the secretary-general of the Australian Olympic Federation, Edgar Tanner, and told him, 'Look, I can't regard these persons as people. What do I do? Become a hypocrite and shake hands with them, or refuse and create an international incident?'

Sir Edgar Tanner had been a POW for three years, and replied that he had more reason to hate them than Philip did. But he intended to be a hypocrite and shake hands.

In the event, Philip shook hands with the Japanese team manager. After just three or four days, he asked himself, 'How can I hate these lovely boys and girls?' He laughed as he recalled that 'the Australian team gave me much more trouble than they did'.

Philip's wartime experiences held one more twist for him. He'd received the surrender of a Japanese officer, Major Saito, who'd handed over to him his sword. Philip had no right to claim it, but he had smuggled the sword back to Australia. Later, he regretted this.

By 1970 Philip was a senior legal officer with the Australian company Conzinc Riotinto, which had an office in Tokyo. Philip found that he had something in common with the Japanese manager: they'd both flown in the Pacific. The Japanese laughingly described himself as a 'failed kamikaze'.

Philip sought his new friend's help in returning the sword—but how to find the major? Saito is a very common Japanese name. The Japanese manager surprised Philip by removing a wooden plug from the handle of the sword to reveal its history inscribed on the haft. He suggested that Philip bring the sword with him the next time he visited Tokyo.

That visit took place when the company was involved in negotiations with the Japanese over the development of the Bougainville copper mine, and Philip recalled that 'negotiations were not going well. The US had applied a tariff barrier on imports and the Japanese were cutting all contracts back by 10 per cent.'

In the midst of these negotiations, Philip received an invitation to appear on television. He assumed that this would be in an attempt to locate a relative of Major Saito, but instead, after a short briefing, he was ushered into a large studio to be greeted by '500 schoolkids, who, when I came in, rose and sang "Waltzing Matilda", and then a young woman was introduced. She was the major's granddaughter, the only surviving member of the family. The only memento they had of the old man was a photo of him with that sword and a little urn of his ashes. In front of a national television audience I formally handed over the sword, and it obviously meant a lot to her.'

And the gesture had wider implications: back at the negotiating table he found that things went much better.

Philip believed that handing back that sword had, for him, 'closed the circle on the Second World War'.

THEY'RE GROWING WHEAT
AT MOUNT HOPE

They're sowing a wheat crop at Mount Hope. That was the story—and if it were true, then it really was a story.

There are optimists in this world, there are super-optimists, and then there's the bloke who named Mount Hope. What he was hoping for is anyone's guess. In that country it could only have been gold.

The locals will tell you that the time Noah had to move his livestock they got half an inch of rain. That's unkind, but the average rainfall is a bit less than four and a half inches a year. It's not what you'd call prime wheat country.

Mount Hope is north of Hillston and south of Cobar in the west of New South Wales. It's just about the edge of the mallee country, but not even the hardiest of the mallee cockies had pushed this far west to sow wheat.

Traditionally, farmers in 'safe' country operated a mixed farming business, using grain and either lamb or wool production as a hedge. If the crop failed, there's always the wool—that was the philosophy. But wool had been on the nose for too long, and some very unlikely country was now seeing the plough. But Mount Hope?

It took me a couple of tries to raise the would-be farmer on the phone, but when I got through he assured me it was true. He was sowing the crop right now, and I could come and have a look if I liked.

I checked. There was a pub in Mount Hope, so accommodation wouldn't be a problem. I was on my way to the farming story of the year.

The received wisdom of the time was: 'If you can get the land cheap enough, you'll make a go of wheat.' It was all about scale of production. Get a big crop in, the argument went, and chances were that in an ordinary year you'd at least get seed back. If you struck one good year in four you'd be in profit.

I thought about that as I headed west. It seemed a logical argument, but it didn't take into account what might happen to the country in a bad year, when you'd get no cover at all.

I've always been interested in the history of this country. I knew that in Henry Lawson's day you could find plenty of references to fattening bullocks on the country around Bourke, and I'd even learned that a hill just outside of Cobar had once been a dairy—a dairy!

I was driving through this country in a bad year—you could flog a flea across the paddocks. What had happened to that dairy and those fat bullocks? The answer was, of course, rabbits. In their plague proportions they'd eaten the country out, and the grass that had fed those bullocks had been replaced by scrub. This is fragile country, but I wasn't thinking of that. I was busting to meet the bloke sowing wheat at Mount Hope.

The first owner of the pub at Mount Hope should be ashamed of himself. How could anyone have so little imagination as to call an iconic bush pub the Royal Hotel? The pub turned out to be a single-storey building with a bar, and that was about it. There was a verandah down the side; I was to get to know that verandah very well.

I approached the bar and introduced myself—I was the bloke who'd rung to arrange accommodation, and to get directions to my would-be farmer's place.

The first shock was to learn that the pub didn't offer accommodation but 'there was a couch out on the verandah. You could unroll your swag there.' That was me for the night. If only I'd brought a swag . . . And so far as directions to my would-be farmer went, all I had to do was follow the road until I came to a dirt track leading off into the mallee scrub. Nothing to it.

Give a true bushman a bit of wire and, with a bullocky twitch, he'll build you anything you like. My would-be wheat farmer was a true bushman. I had expected to find him in a worked-up paddock—he was, after all, sowing wheat. No.

His basic farming implement was a Caterpillar D8, the sort of heavy bulldozer that was usually used in this part of the country for tank sinking, and he was making it work.

Hitched to the D8 was a plough, hitched to the plough was a cultivator, hitched to the cultivator was a combine seeder, and hitched to the combine was a covering harrows. He was ploughing the country, cultivating it and sowing all in one pass. I couldn't wait to see him turn a corner.

The size and shape of the paddock was the next surprise. He was working country that had been cleared of mallee scrub but he wasn't sowing the whole lot.

'No,' he told me with a perfectly straight face. 'I just drive in that direction for a quarter of an hour, and then I turn around and come back.'

That's the way you sow a wheat crop at Mount Hope.

With that story safe in the recorder, I headed back to the Royal and my couch for the night. There was one more unique experience in store for me.

The locals had come to town for a celebration. Thinking back, I'm pretty sure that the occasion was the retirement of the local postmaster or postmistress. They were leaving the district, and a send-off was in order.

They were a great, friendly bunch, and the night progressed and progressed, and then I saw something I doubt you'd see anywhere else in the world. The publican wished the retiree well and announced that he was going to bed—goodnight. He took the big money out of the till behind the bar and left the premises. The party continued.

As drinks were required, someone would wander behind the bar, pour the drinks, collect the necessary cash, ring up the amount and pop it in the till. And that was still going on when I pulled stumps and headed for that couch on the verandah.

These days, I note, the Royal is the only visible business in town, and the surrounding mallee scrub is prized for the preservation of malleefowl and red-lored whistler. The wheat crop didn't make it.

COUNTRY FOOTBALL'S
GONE TO BUGGERY

I PICKED UP THIS STORY IN A LITTLE TOWN IN THE VICTORIAN MALLEE. I'd gone into a pub to ask for directions and come face to face with club memorabilia. The pub obviously sponsored the town team. There were pictures everywhere, but pride of place was given to an old jumper in a glass frame. The jumper was so caked in mud that you could only guess at its colour. There had to be a story there.

'That's from the 1956 grand final,' the old bloke behind the bar told me. 'You remember—the wet year.'

It turned out that back when football was played by men, the big rivals in the local league were the town team, the Blues, and a team from the local mission, the Boomerangs—or Rangs, as they were known. The Rangs had won back-to-back grand finals, and the townies were determined that '56 would be their year. They'd gone undefeated all season, while the Rangs had finished fourth and fought their way through the semis to make the big one.

The Rangs were led by their centre half-forward, a massive bloke who, the barman assured me, 'coulda got a game anywhere. The big teams in Melbourne was chasin' him but he wouldn't leave. Didn't want to have to play in boots.'

It seemed that this big bloke always played in bare feet. There were unkind people who suggested that this was because you couldn't find boots that would fit him.

'He had a bloody good grip on Australia, that's for certain,' my informant told me.

Came grand final day and it was 'raining an inch a minute', I was told. 'Something you don't see too often around here. Well, comes time for the teams to run through the banners, and the Rangs are a couple short. They ask for an extra ten minutes to round up a team, and the captain of the Blues, a nice bloke, agrees. Two skinny fourteen-year-olds turn up, pull on the boots and the game's away.

'Like I said, it's rainin' an inch a minute, so it's wet-weather footy, not pretty but tough. Long story short, the Blues are in front in the last quarter but the Rangs are comin' hard. The crowd's off its head. Never seen a game like it. Rain still beltin' down so hard you can't make out who's who on the paddock.

'The Rangs kick one, and that gets 'em to within a point, but there's only seconds to go. If they're gonna win, the ball's gotta come straight outta the centre, someone's gotta take a big mark and then kick a goal.

'The Blues have packed the backline, but out comes the ball—and the big bloke from the Rangs goes up and takes a screamer. The siren sounds. Now, if he kicks this the Rangs win, if he kicks a point it's a draw, and if he misses the Blues have got it. No one in the crowd's breathin'. It's dead quiet.

'He turns round to have a look, and you can hardly see the goals, it's rainin' that hard. Well, he puts the ball down and starts to scoop up a big turkey nest of mud. He's gonna place-kick it. Nobody's done a place kick for years.

'Back he goes. He wipes the mud off his big, broad, bare foot and runs in five steps. Smack! You could hear the sound all over the ground. Well, the ball flies through the air. The Blues have got their ruckman in the goal square but it's no use—the ball sails over the top of 'is head. The ump waves the two flags and the Rangs have won back-to-back-to-back.

'The boys are back here cryin' in their beer, and they get to arguing about that kick. I mean, with rain all day, that ball's gotta be as heavy as lead, and he musta kicked it 50 yards.

'Someone says they should measure the kick, so everyone's back down the ground with a tape measure. The turkey's nest's still there, of course, so they can measure from that—but, bugger me, there's the ball still sittin' on the mound. He hasn't kicked it at all. But 50 yards, two feet, nine inches away, between the big sticks, is a little mallee root. He's grubbed 'er out and kicked 'er that far with his bare foot. That's his jumper up there.

'Ah, country footy's gone to buggery these days.'

'85 8 20

ACKNOWLEDGEMENTS

I'D LIKE TO ACKNOWLEDGE MY DEBT TO NEIL INALL, A CHAMPION OF regional broadcasting, a true friend and the inspiration behind the program *All Ways on Sunday*. It was Neil's enthusiasm that led to the pilot for the program and Graham White's foresight that turned what could have been just another half-hour radio program into what it became.

We could say that the program was a happy accident, something that turned up at the right time in the right place, but that would be selling Graham short. He realised the great opportunity we had to record the voices of Australia at a time of rapid change. Before oral history became a 'buzz' word, Graham recognised the power of radio to capture the unique voice of the country. It was he who supported the move to have a national radio program broadcast from a regional station. It had never been done before and it gave the program the flexibility it needed to rove to so many parts of the country. I need particularly to thank Graham for the courage he showed in supporting me during the early days of the program when I was truly terrible. Thank heavens I learned.

All Ways on Sunday would not have been possible without the network of rural reporters across the country whose contributions to the program gave it its flavour and of course to the many hundreds of people who contributed their stories. The program was a hungry beast and without their continuing support it could never have continued. To all those listeners who welcomed me into their homes on Sunday morning, thank you. It was a privilege I treasure.

I learned my craft at 2CR in Orange and owe a debt to so many people there. I've written about some of them in this book, but they and literally hundreds of the station's regular listeners became family. The station welcomed me twice, once as a raw rural trainee and much later as its manager. There I was blessed with some of the most talented broadcasters you're ever likely to meet. Their light may have been hidden under the bushel of regional radio but they had the talent to match any of their high-flying capital-city counterparts. Together we had great pride in the station and a true dedication to serve the people in 2CR country. The station motto was 'I'm proud to own 2CR' and we meant it with all our hearts.

I've been urged many times to write some of the stories I collected in *All Ways on Sunday* but I resisted until Craig Alexander, a young actor I'd worked with, encouraged me to re-tell some of them in a one-man show. I thought I was past it but his encouragement got me onto the stage one last time. Richard Walsh, my publisher at Allen & Unwin, read the script for that show and encouraged me to further efforts. I need to thank them both for what became a very pleasant experience.

Despite what some of my former colleagues will tell you, I don't adhere to the adage 'never let the facts get in the way of a good story', but none of the stories told in *All Ways on Sunday* were saved—what we have here is the memory of an eighty-year-old brain. If I've blurred some of the facts please forgive me.

PHOTO CREDITS

Internal images courtesy of: ABC Central West/Melanie Pearce (p. 3, 2CR transmitter at Cumnock; p. 5, Laurie Mulhall), Charles Bayliss/National Library of Australia (p. 43, Dunlop Station), Neil Inall (p. 75, Graham White and Neil Inall), unknown (p. 82, Holtermann nugget), Charles Mountford/State Library of South Australia (p. 136, Bob Buck), State Library of Western Australia (p. 145, Gloucester Tree), Australian Broadcasting Corporation (p. 197, Ruth Cracknell and Alex Nicol), Fairfax Media/National Library of Australia (p. 203, Randwick Racecourse), Alex Nicol (p. 217, 2CR T-shirt with logo by Stephen Nicol), unknown (p. 242, Alex Nicol shearing), unknown (p. 258, Alex Nicol in the 2CR studio).